TEACHER'S PET PUBLICATIONS

LITPLAN TEACHER PACK
for
Black Boy
based on the book by
Richard Wright

Written by
Mary B. Collins

© 1999 Teacher's Pet Publications
All Rights Reserved

This **LitPlan** for Richard Wright's
Black Boy
has been brought to you by Teacher's Pet Publications, Inc.

Copyright Teacher's Pet Publications 1999
11504 Hammock Point
Berlin MD 21811

Only the student materials in this unit plan
such as worksheets, study questions, assignment sheets, and tests
may be reproduced multiple times for use in the purchaser's classroom.

For any additional copyright questions,
contact Teacher's Pet Publications.

www.tpet.com

TABLE OF CONTENTS - *Black Boy*

Introduction	5
Unit Objectives	7
Reading Assignment Sheet	8
Unit Outline	9
Study Questions (Short Answer)	13
Quiz/Study Questions (Multiple Choice)	22
Pre-reading Vocabulary Worksheets	41
Lesson One (Introductory Lesson)	59
Nonfiction Assignment Sheet	61
Oral Reading Evaluation Form	63
Writing Assignment 1	65
Writing Assignment 2	71
Writing Assignment 3	78
Writing Evaluation Form	81
Vocabulary Review Activities	75
Extra Writing Assignments/Discussion ?s	73
Unit Review Activities	83
Unit Tests	87
Unit Resource Materials	121
Vocabulary Resource Materials	135

A FEW NOTES ABOUT THE AUTHOR
Richard Wright

WRIGHT, Richard (1908-1960). The American author Richard Wright pictured with brutal realism what it meant to be black in a white society. His writings speak with the raw voice of an anguish not often evident in novels.

Richard Nathaniel Wright was born on Sept. 4, 1908, on a plantation near Natchez, Mississippi. His father was a mill hand, and his mother taught in a country school. Young Wright's childhood was generally one of poverty, frustration, and despair. When he was 5, his father left the family, and when he was not yet 10, his mother became paralyzed. He was sent to live with relatives. At 15 he left home and for several years drifted from one city to another, working at whatever jobs he could find. In Chicago he worked nights in the post office. Days he spent reading and writing. During the depression of the 1930's, he lost his job and had to go on relief. Not long afterward he joined the Communist party, as did thousands of other young Americans at the time.

In 1937 Wright moved to New York City, where he worked on a Federal Writers' Project. His first published book, *Uncle Tom's Children*, appeared in 1938. It was a collection of four stories dealing with racial prejudice and violence in the South. But it was Wright's novel *Black Boy* (1940) that brought him world fame. This powerful story of a Chicago black driven to crime was made into a play by Wright and Paul Green. It was successfully staged in 1941.

Wright's first marriage--to a ballet dancer--ended in divorce. In 1941 he married Ellen Poplar of New York City, and they had two daughters. Wright became increasingly disillusioned with the Communist party and finally left it. In 1945 he published *Black Boy*, an autobiography of his childhood and youth. It confirmed him as a major American writer.

His discontent with American society persisted. As a youth he had experienced not only hardship but vicious racial prejudice as well, and as a man he continued to encounter it. In 1946 he and his white wife left the United States to live in Paris.

Wright wrote several novels during the next 14 years, but they were not well received. He also wrote some travel books and other nonfiction. On November 28, 1960, he died in Paris of a heart attack.

---- Courtesy of Compton's Learning Company

INTRODUCTION

This unit has been designed to develop students' reading, writing, thinking, and language skills through exercises and activities related to *Black Boy* by Richard Wright. It includes eighteen lessons, supported by extra resource materials.

The **introductory lesson** introduces students to some background to the novel through a writing and bulletin board activity. Following the introductory activity, students are given a transition to explain how the activity relates to the book they are about to read. Following the transition, students are given the materials they will be using during the unit. At the end of the lesson, students begin the pre-reading work for the first reading assignment.

The **reading assignments** are approximately thirty pages in length. Some are a little shorter and others are a little longer depending on where the chapter divisions are. Students have approximately 20 minutes of pre-reading work to do prior to each reading assignment. This pre-reading work involves reviewing the study questions for the assignment and doing some vocabulary work for 8 to 10 vocabulary words they will encounter in their reading.

The **study guide questions** are fact-based questions; students can find the answers to these questions right in the text. These questions come in two formats: short answer or multiple choice. The best use of these materials is probably to use the short answer version of the questions as study guides for students (since answers will be more complete), and to use the multiple choice version for occasional quizzes. If your school has the appropriate equipment, it might be a good idea to make transparencies of your answer keys for the overhead projector.

The **vocabulary work** is intended to enrich students' vocabularies as well as to aid in the students' understanding of the book. Prior to each reading assignment, students will complete a two-part worksheet for approximately 8 to 10 vocabulary words in the upcoming reading assignment. Part I focuses on students' use of general knowledge and contextual clues by giving the sentence in which the word appears in the text. Students are then to write down what they think the words mean based on the words' usage. Part II nails down the definitions of the words by giving students dictionary definitions of the words and having students match the words to the correct definitions based on the words' contextual usage. Students should then have a thorough understanding of the words when they meet them in the text.

After each reading assignment, students will go back and formulate answers for the study guide questions. Discussion of these questions serves as a **review** of the most important events and ideas presented in the reading assignments.

After students complete reading the work, there is a **vocabulary review** lesson which pulls together all of the fragmented vocabulary lists for the reading assignments and gives students a review of all of the words they have studied.

A lesson is devoted to the **extra discussion questions/writing assignments**. These questions focus on interpretation, critical analysis and personal response, employing a variety of thinking skills and adding to the students' understanding of the novel.

There is a **group activity** in which students work in small groups to discuss symbolism, imagery and themes from the novel.

The group activity is followed by a **reports and discussion** session in which the groups share their ideas about the themes with the entire class; thus, the entire class is exposed to information about all of the themes and the entire class can discuss each theme based on the nucleus of information brought forth by each of the groups.

There are three **writing assignments** in this unit, each with the purpose of informing, persuading, or having students express personal opinions. The first assignment is to have students express their own opinions: students write a composition in which they tell what ideas and themes they think Richard Wright would put in a book called *Black Boy* today. The second assignment is to inform: students write a report in which they organize and compose the information they plan to give for their oral presentations relating to the **unit project**. The third assignment is to persuade: students write a persuasive composition of their own choice.

The **unit project** is in five parts. Students are assigned one of the authors Richard mentions after he has read the Mencken books. Students take the author, find out what Mencken said about the author, read biographical information about the author, read something the author has written, and read some critics' articles evaluating the author's work. Following the research and the related writing assignment, students each give an oral presentation. This project also doubles as a **nonfiction reading assignment**.

The **review lesson** pulls together all of the aspects of the unit. The teacher is given four or five choices of activities or games to use which all serve the same basic function of reviewing all of the information presented in the unit.

The **unit test** comes in two formats: multiple choice or short answer. As a convenience, two different tests for each format have been included. There is also an advanced short answer test for students who need more of a challenge.

There are additional **support materials** included with this unit. The **extra activities section** includes suggestions for an in-class library, crossword and word search puzzles related to the novel, and extra vocabulary worksheets. There is a list of **bulletin board ideas** which gives the teacher suggestions for bulletin boards to go along with this unit. In addition, there is a list of **extra class activities** the teacher could choose from to enhance the unit or as a substitution for an exercise the teacher might feel is inappropriate for his/her class. **Answer keys** are located directly after the **reproducible student materials** throughout the unit. Only the student materials may be reproduced for use in the teacher's classroom without infringement of copyrights.

UNIT OBJECTIVES - *Black Boy*

1. Through reading *Black Boy* students will consider the importance of judging people as individuals rather than as members of groups.

2. Students will demonstrate their understanding of the text on four levels: factual, interpretive, critical and personal.

3. Students will study the theme of man's search for his own identity and the conflicts within himself as well as those imposed by society.

4. Students will be given the opportunity to practice reading aloud and silently to improve their skills in each area.

5. Students will answer questions to demonstrate their knowledge and understanding of the main events and characters in *Black Boy* as they relate to the author's theme development.

6. Students will enrich their vocabularies and improve their understanding of the novel through the vocabulary lessons prepared for use in conjunction with the novel.

7. The writing assignments in this unit are geared to several purposes:
    a. To have students demonstrate their abilities to inform, to persuade, or to express their own personal ideas
        NOTE: Students will demonstrate ability to write effectively to <u>inform</u> by developing and organizing facts to convey information. Students will demonstrate the ability to write effectively to <u>persuade</u> by selecting and organizing relevant information, establishing an argumentative purpose, and by designing an appropriate strategy for an identified audience. Students will demonstrate the ability to write effectively to <u>express personal ideas</u> by selecting a form and its appropriate elements.
    b. To check the students' reading comprehension
    c. To make students think about the ideas presented by the novel
    d. To encourage logical thinking
    e. To provide an opportunity to practice good grammar and improve students' use of the English language.

8. Students will read aloud, report, and participate in large and small group discussions to improve their public speaking and personal interaction skills.

READING ASSIGNMENT SHEET - *Black Boy*

Date Assigned	Assignment	Completion Date
	1	
	2	
	3	
	4	
	5-6	
	7-8	
	9-11	
	12-14	

UNIT OUTLINE - *Black Boy*

1 Introduction PV 1	2 Read 1 PV 2	3 Study ?s 1 Read 2 PV 3	4 Study ?s 2 Read 3 PVR 4	5 Study ?s 3 Writing Assignment #1 PVR 5-6
6 Library - Nonfiction Reading	7 Study ?s 4-6 Project Work PVR 7-8	8 Study ?s 7-8 Writing Assignment #2 PVR 9-11	9 Study ?s 9-11 PVR 12-14	10 Study ?s 12-14 Extra ?s
11 Vocabulary	12 Group Activity	13 Group Reports & Discussion	14 Nonfiction Reports	15 Nonfiction Reports
16 Writing Assignment #3	17 Review	18 Test		

P=Preview Study Questions V=Prereading Vocabulary Worksheets R=Read

STUDY GUIDE QUESTIONS

SHORT ANSWER STUDY GUIDE QUESTIONS - *Black Boy*

Chapter 1
1. Who is the narrator?
2. Why did little Richard set the house on fire?
3. What happened to little Richard as punishment for setting the fire?
4. How and why did Richard kill the kitten?
5. Why did Richard's mother make him go to the store even though she knew he might be beaten again?
6. Why was Richard always hungry?
7. What did Richard do to pass the time of day when he was six years old?
8. How did Richard learn to count, and what did he learn in his first day of school?
9. What happened in court, and what effect did it have on Richard's attitude towards his father?
10. Why did Richard have to go to an orphans' home?
11. Why did Mrs. Wright and Richard go to see Mr. Wright? What happened?
12. How did Richard describe his father at the end of the chapter, in retrospect?

Chapter 2
1. Why didn't Granny want Richard to read story books?
2. Why did Granny hit Richard with a wet towel? Why does his punishment seem unjust to him?
3. On the trip to Arkansas, Richard becomes more aware of the separations between blacks and whites. When he asks his mother questions about racial differences, what is her reaction to him?
4. What happened to Uncle Hoskins? Why?
5. What two groups of men did Richard see when he and his mother and aunt returned to Granny's?
6. Why did the Wrights have to move again soon after they got to West Helena?
7. Why were Aunt Maggie and "uncle" forced to leave?
8. What was ironic about Betsy's death?

Chapters 3-4
1. Why did Richard move to Greenwood with Uncle Clark and Aunt Jody?
2. What fear forced Richard to ask to leave Greenwood?
3. What effect did Richard's mother's illness have on him?
4. Who was Granny's ally in trying to make Richard get religion?
5. Why did Addie beat Richard, and what was his reaction?
6. How did Granny get embarrassed in church?
7. Why did Richard write his first story?

Black Boy Short Answer Study Questions Page 2

Chapters 5-6
1. How did Richard's family react to his sixth grade promotion?
2. Why did Richard sell the anti-Negro newspapers?
3. Why did Addie say she would kill Richard?
4. Who was Brother Manse, and what did Richard gain from his job with him?
5. How did Addie and Granny react to Grandpa's death?
6. What was Richard's mother's reaction to his defiance of Granny and Addie and their consequent consent to his working?
7. Why didn't Richard want to work for the white woman who gave him moldy molasses?
8. Why did Richard begin attending Sunday school?
9. Why did Richard finally consent to being baptized into the church?
10. Why did Richard threaten to cut his Uncle Tom with razors?

Chapters 7-8
1. What was The Voodoo of Hell's Half-Acre?
2. What did the North symbolize for Richard?
3. What effect did the death of Ned's brother, Bob, have on Richard?
4. Why did Richard refuse to deliver the pre-written graduation speech?

Chapters 9-11
1. What three incidents left an impression on Richard during his time working at the clothing store?
2. What advice did Griggs give Richard?
3. Why did Richard quit working at the optical company?
4. Describe Mr. Crane's attitude towards Richard.
5. How did Richard get enough money to go North?
6. Why did Richard resort to crime?
7. Who was Mrs. Moss? Bess?
8. What plans did Mrs. Moss have for Richard?
9. Why did Richard refuse Bess?

Chapters 12-14
1. Identify Shorty.
2. Why did Richard fight Harrison?
3. What was the result of the fight?
4. What author/editor intrigued Richard?
5. How did Richard manage to get books from the library?
6. What effect did the books have on Richard?
7. How did Richard finally get to go North from Memphis?

ANSWER KEY SHORT ANSWER STUDY GUIDE QUESTIONS - *Black Boy*

Chapter 1

1. Who is the narrator?
   Richard Wright is the narrator; the book is an autobiography.

2. Why did little Richard set the house on fire?
   He was playing with fire and just wanted to see what the curtains would look like as they were burning. It was indirectly an accident.

3. What happened to little Richard as punishment for setting the fire?
   His mother almost beat him to death. He was very ill following the beating.

4. How and why did Richard kill the kitten?
   Richard hanged the kitten. His father, in anger and trying to get some peace and quiet so he could sleep, told the boys to kill the kitten. He didn't mean it literally, but Richard did kill the kitten as a way of hitting back at his father and showing his hatred.

5. Why did Richard's mother make him go to the store even though she knew he might be beaten again?
   She was teaching him to stand up for himself--to fight back and survive in the real world.

6. Why was Richard always hungry?
   His father left home. Although his mother worked, she couldn't earn enough money to provide shelter and all the food and clothes the boys needed. Later when she became ill, hunger was even more of a problem.

7. What did Richard do to pass the time of day when he was six years old?
   He went to the local saloon where people bought him drinks and urged him to repeat obscenities.

8. How did Richard learn to count, and what did he learn in his first day of school?
   The coal man taught him to count. On the first day of school he learned lots of four-letter words, which he soaped on the neighbors' windows when he got home.

9. What happened in court, and what effect did it have on Richard's attitude towards his father?
   Mrs. Wright and the boys went to court to try to get more child support from Mr. Wright. Mr. Wright smiled and lied to the judge, saying he was doing all he could. The judge ruled in his favor. Richard saw the injustice and lost any respect he had had for his father. He didn't want to see his father any more.

10. Why did Richard have to go to an orphans' home?
    His mother became ill and could no longer support him.

11. Why did Mrs. Wright and Richard go to see Mr. Wright? What happened?
    They went to ask him for money so they could move to live with Mrs. Wright's sister. The point was to get Richard out of the orphanage. They found Mr. Wright with another woman. He refused to give Richard anything but a nickel of charity, which Richard refused.

12. How did Richard describe his father at the end of the chapter, in retrospect?
    "... my father was a black peasant who had gone to the city seeking life, but who had failed in the city; a black peasant whose life had been hopelessly snarled in the city, and who had at last fled the city -- ...."

Chapter 2

1. Why didn't Granny want Richard to read story books?
    She was a very religious woman who believed all pleasurable things were sinful, that one would burn in hell for enjoying anything.

2. Why did Granny hit Richard with a wet towel? Why does his punishment seem unjust to him?
    Richard told Granny she could "kiss back there" when she finished scrubbing him. Granny took great offense at such "obscenities" being said to her, so she beat him (and so did his mother later). He didn't realize the meaning of the words he had said, so his punishment seemed unfair to him.

3. On the trip to Arkansas, Richard becomes more aware of the separations between blacks and whites. When he asks his mother questions about racial differences, what is her reaction to him?
    She brushed his questions off with a few bare facts. He later said, "She was not concealing facts, but feelings, attitudes, convictions, which she did not want me to know."

4. What happened to Uncle Hoskins? Why?
    White men shot him because he would not heed their threats. They were jealous of his flourishing liquor business.

5. What two groups of men did Richard see when he and his mother and aunt returned to Granny's?
    He saw soldiers and prisoners.

6. Why did the Wrights have to move again soon after they got to West Helena?
    They had unknowingly moved in next to a whore house. Richard's peeking into the room next door led to an argument with the landlady, and she told them to leave.

7. Why were Aunt Maggie and "uncle" forced to leave?
   "Uncle" had done something and the white people were after him.

8. What was ironic about Betsy's death?
   Richard tried to sell her to a white woman, but then he refused to sell her because of his anxieties about white people. A week later the dog was run over in his own neighborhood. He then did not have the dog or the money.

Chapters 3-4

1. Why did Richard move to Greenwood with Uncle Clark and Aunt Jody?
   His mother had a stroke, and the children had to move in with relatives. Richard chose to live with Uncle Clark because Greenwood was the choice nearest to his mother.

2. What fear forced Richard to ask to leave Greenwood?
   He found out that a boy had died in the bed in which he slept at Uncle Clark's house. That made him afraid to sleep in the bed, and Aunt Jody and Uncle Clark would not let him sleep anywhere else. He became exhausted and could not get along living there anymore.

3. What effect did Richard's mother's illness have on him?
   "My mother's suffering grew into a symbol in my mind, gathering to itself all the poverty, the ignorance, the helplessness; the painful, baffling, hunger-ridden days and hours; the restless moving, the futile seeking, the uncertainty, the fear, the dread; the meaningless pain and the endless suffering. Her life set the emotional tone of my life, colored the men and women I was to meet in the future, conditioned my relation to events that had not yet happened, determined my attitude to situations and circumstances I had yet to face. A somberness of spirit that I was never to lose settled over me during the slow years of my mother's unrelieved suffering, a somberness that was to make me stand apart and look upon excessive joy with suspicion, that was to make me self-conscious, that was to make me keep forever on the move, as though to escape a nameless fate seeking to overtake me."

4. Who was Granny's ally in trying to make Richard get religion?
   Aunt Addie was her ally.

5. Why did Addie beat Richard, and what was his reaction?
   She had a preconceived notion that he was a bad boy--from things she had heard in the family. At school she assumed he lied to her about the nuts. When he tried to defend himself, she grew angrier. At home she tried to beat him as additional punishment for his infractions at school, but Richard refused to be beaten unjustly. He defended himself with a knife, and Addie left him alone.

6. How did Granny get embarrassed in church?
    Richard whispered to her that if he had seen an angel like Jacob had, he would believe, too. Granny misunderstood and told the preacher that Richard had seen an angel. When things got out of hand, Richard confessed that he had said "IF," and he scolded Granny in front of other members of her church.

7. Why did Richard write his first story?
    He was bored with prayer when he thought of the idea, and writing it gave him an escape from his oppressive life.

Chapters 5-6

1. How did Richard's family react to his sixth grade promotion?
    "The family had not thought it possible. How could a bad, bad boy do that?"

2. Why did Richard sell the anti-Negro newspapers?
    He did not know the content of the papers; he just wanted to read the magazine section of stories and to make a little money.

3. Why did Addie say she would kill Richard?
    Instead of recognizing that Granny fell because Richard dodged an unjust blow, Addie blamed Richard for Granny's accident. By that point she was so furious with him for other infractions that she flew into a rage with this latest provocation and swore she would kill him.

4. Who was Brother Manse, and what did Richard gain from his job with him?
    Brother Manse was Richard's next-door neighbor who gave him the job of reading and writing for him in his insurance work. In his travels with Brother Manse, Richard gained a new outlook on life and a little self-respect.

5. How did Addie and Granny react to Grandpa's death?
    They showed no emotion--no tears. They dealt with his death in a rather cold, factual manner. "The routine of the house flowed on as usual."

6. What was Richard's mother's reaction to his defiance of Granny and Addie and their consequent consent to his working?
    ". . . my mother smiled. . . . She rose and hobbled to me on her paralytic legs and kissed me. . . ."

7. Why didn't Richard want to work for the white woman who gave him moldy molasses?
    "The woman had assaulted my ego; she had assumed that she knew my place in life, what I felt, what I ought to be, and I resented it with all my heart."

8. Why did Richard begin attending Sunday school?
   He went to talk and be with his friends.

9. Why did Richard finally consent to being baptized into the church?
   He did it out of love for his mother, not love of God. He didn't want his mother to be humiliated.

10. Why did Richard threaten to cut his Uncle Tom with razors?
    Tom had, from Richard's viewpoint, unjustly threatened to beat him. Richard was determined that no one would beat him when he felt in his heart that he had done nothing wrong.

Chapters 7-8
1. What was The Voodoo of Hell's Half-Acre?
   It was the first story that Richard wrote for publication. He had wanted it to make him more acceptable to his school mates, but it alienated them from him. He received criticism for it at home, even from his mother.

2. What did the North symbolize for Richard?
   "The North symbolized to me all that I had not felt and seen; it had no relation whatever to what actually existed. Yet, by imagining a place where everything was possible, I kept hope alive in me."

3. What effect did the death of Ned's brother, Bob, have on Richard?
   "What I had heard altered the look of the world. . . . The penalty of death awaited me if I made a false move and I wondered if it was worth-while to make any move at all.'

4. Why did Richard refuse to deliver the pre-written graduation speech?
   He "didn't want to do things that way." He felt that his speech as Valedictorian should be his own instead of a piece prepared by others for social or political reasons.

Chapters 9-11
1. What three incidents left an impression on Richard during his time working at the clothing store?
   He saw a black woman raped by his bosses and saw that the white policeman sided with the white bosses. White boys hit him with a bottle and knocked him off the running board for not saying, "Sir." Policemen stopped him, searched him, and told him to tell his boss not to send him to white neighborhoods late at night.

2. What advice did Griggs give Richard?
   "When you're in front of white people, think before you act, think before you speak. Your way of doing things is all right among our people, but not for white people. They won't stand for it."

3. Why did Richard quit working at the optical company?
    Pease and Reynolds, two white employees, ganged up on him and threatened to kill him if he told the boss about their abuse of him.

4. Describe Mr. Crane's attitude towards Richard.
    Crane was a good-hearted white man from the North. He sincerely wanted to help Richard, but even he could not help within the pervasive constraints of Southern culture.

5. How did Richard get enough money to go North?
    He took a job at a movie house and took part in a scheme which skimmed money from ticket sales there.

6. Why did Richard resort to crime?
    He lived in fear of saying or doing the wrong thing, which might get him killed in the South, so he felt the need to get away as quickly as possible. However, his jobs did not pay enough for him to live and save money. He felt as though he had no choice but to resort to crime.

7. Who was Mrs. Moss? Bess?
    Mrs. Moss was a woman who had rooms for rent in Memphis. Bess was her daughter. Richard stayed with them when he went to Memphis.

8. What plans did Mrs. Moss have for Richard?
    She wanted Richard to marry Bess.

9. Why did Richard refuse Bess?
    He was overwhelmed by her simple offer of love, he did not love her, and he worried about his responsibilities if she would get pregnant; he might be trapped again before realizing his dream of living in the North.

Chapters 12-14
1. Identify Shorty.
    Shorty was a young black boy who operated the elevator in the building where Richard worked. Shorty did not have the personal honor that Richard had. He would do almost anything for money, including letting a white man kick him for a quarter.

2. Why did Richard fight Harrison?
    Mr. Olin and other white men convinced Richard that Harrison was out to get him and convinced Harrison that Richard was out to get him. Even though the two boys met and honestly told each other that they had no malice towards each other, they still couldn't totally trust each other. Finally, the boys decided to fight under the agreement that they wouldn't really hurt each other; they would just pretend.

3. What was the result of the fight?
    The boys' agreement was forgotten, and both fought until they were exhausted. Richard said, "I felt that I had done something unclean, something for which I could never properly atone."

4. What author/editor intrigued Richard?
    He liked H. L. Mencken.

5. How did Richard manage to get books from the library?
    He made arrangements with a Catholic white man at work, Mr. Falk, to pretend to be sent from Falk to get books from the library.

6. What effect did the books have on Richard?
    They provided an escape, gave him hope, and helped to educate him.

7. How did Richard finally get to go North from Memphis?
    He saved his money. He and his aunt were to go and find a place to stay, and they were to send for his mother and brother when things were ready.

MULTIPLE CHOICE STUDY GUIDE/QUIZ QUESTIONS - *Black Boy*

Chapter 1

1. To which genre does this work belong?
   - A. It is a biography.
   - B. It is a play.
   - C. It is an autobiography.
   - D. It is historical fiction.

2. Why did little Richard set the house on fire?
   - A. It was an accident. He was playing and wanted to see what the curtains would look like if they were burning.
   - B. His brother offered to pay him fifty cents if he would do it.
   - C. He was trying out something he had seen at the movies.
   - D. He was angry at his mother and wanted to burn down the house.

3. What happened to little Richard as punishment for setting the fire?
   - A. His father held his hands in the fire and gave him severe burns that left life-long scars.
   - B. His mother almost beat him to death. He was very ill afterwards.
   - C. His parents locked him in his room for three days without food.
   - D. His parents made him get a job delivering papers to start paying for repairs.

4. How did Richard kill the kitten?
   - A. He burned it.
   - B. He stoned it.
   - C. He drowned it.
   - D. He hanged it.

5. Why did Richard kill the kitten?
   - A. He took his father's command literally and did it as a way of getting back at his father and showing his hatred.
   - B. The cat was getting more attention at home than he was and he was jealous. Then when the cat scratched him, he lost his temper and killed it.
   - C. He was starving because his parents didn't have enough money for food. He was planning to eat it.
   - D. He had to do it to be accepted into the street gang he wanted to join.

6. Why did Richard's mother make him go to the store even though she knew he might be beaten again?
   - A. She was desperate for food but was afraid to go to the store herself.
   - B. She subconsciously hoped he would be killed so that she would not have to take care of him any more.
   - C. She was teaching him to stand up for himself, to survive in the real world.
   - D. She was drunk and didn't realize what she was doing.

Black Boy-Multiple Choice Study/Quiz Questions Page 2

7. Why was Richard always hungry?
    A. He had an extra-fast metabolism. He actually needed medical treatment, but his parents didn't know how to go about getting it.
    B. His father left home. His mother worked but didn't make enough money to feed and shelter them. Then she became ill and wasn't able to support them at all.
    C. His family didn't like him. They treated his younger brother much better and even gave him half of Richard's food so that he would be strong. They didn't really care if Richard lived or died.
    D. He refused to eat with the family out of anger and resentment. After a while, the family simply stopped expecting him at the table. He was forced to grab whatever leftovers he could find in the kitchen.

8. What did Richard do to pass the time of day when he was six years old?
    A. He went to the local saloon where people bought him drinks and urged him to repeat obscenities.
    B. He beat up the younger children in the neighborhood and stole their food.
    C. He hid out in the library and taught himself to read.
    D. He visited the elderly neighbors and begged for food.

9. How did Richard learn to count?
    A. One of the storekeepers liked him and taught him.
    B. He watched and listened to the older boys throwing dice and playing cards.
    C. He learned by watching game shows on television.
    D. The coal man taught him when he delivered the coal.

10. What did Richard learn on his first day of school?
    A. He learned lots of four letter words, which he soaped on the neighbor's windows when he got home.
    B. He learned how to write his name.
    C. He learned the route to school and back, so he could walk by himself.
    D. He learned the names of all of the students in his class.

11. What happened in court?
    A. The judge ruled in the mother's favor.
    B. The judge ruled in the father's favor.
    C. The case was held over.
    D. The judge refused to make a ruling.

Black Boy-Multiple Choice Study/Quiz Questions Page 3

12. What effects did it have on Richard's attitude towards his father?
    A. He felt sorry for his father.
    B. He lost respect for his father.
    C. He lived by himself on the streets.
    D. He went to live in an orphanage.

13. What happened to Richard when his mother became ill?
    A. He went to reform school.
    B. He went to live with his father.
    C. He lived by himself on the streets.
    D. He went to live in an orphanage.

14. Where did Mrs. Wright and Richard go when she was feeling a bit better?
    A. They went back to court to try and get more money from Mr. Wright.
    B. They went to Mr. Wright's parents to ask for their help.
    C. They went to Mr. Wright's home to ask him for money.
    D. They went to visit Mr. Wright in jail.

15. What happened?
    A. He offered them ten dollars a month.
    B. The other woman beat Mrs. Wright.
    C. He offered Richard a nickel, which he refused.
    D. He threatened to kill them if they didn't leave.

16. How did Richard describe his father at the end of the chapter, in retrospect?
    A. "A black peasant"
    B. "A drunken bum"
    C. "A sad, broken man"
    D. "A pathetic symbol of all that was wrong with black men"

Black Boy-Multiple Choice Study/Quiz Questions Page 4

Chapter 2

17. What didn't Granny want Richard to do, because of her religious beliefs?
    A. She didn't want him to eat meat.
    B. She didn't want him to read story books.
    C. She didn't want him to talk to girls.
    D. She didn't want him to stay in bed late on Sundays.

18. Why did Granny hit Richard with a wet towel?
    A. He threatened to hit her.
    B. He told her something that she thought was obscene.
    C. He refused to let her wash him.
    D. He was splashing water and laughing.

19. How did he feel about his punishment?
    A. He thought it was fair, that he deserved it.
    B. He thought it was unfair; he didn't even realize that what he had done was wrong.
    C. He thought he should never be punished.
    D. He thought that young people should never be disciplined.

20. On the trip to Arkansas, Richard becomes more aware of the separations between blacks and whites. When he asks his mother questions about racial differences, what is her reaction to him?
    A. She quietly and calmly tells him everything she knows.
    B. She ignores him and refuses to answer at all.
    C. She brushed his questions off with a few bare facts.
    D. She tells him there are no differences, that the idea is all in his imagination.

21. What happened to Uncle Hoskins?
    A. White men who were jealous of his successful business shot him.
    B. He had a heart attack and died in the store.
    C. He went bankrupt, had to give up the store, and committed suicide.
    D. He got in the middle of a barroom brawl and was stabbed to death.

22. What groups of men did Richard see when he, his mother, and aunt returned to Granny's?
    A. He saw sailors and students.
    B. He saw prisoners and students.
    C. He saw soldiers and sailors.
    D. He saw prisoners and soldiers.

Black Boy-Multiple Choice Study/Quiz Questions Page 5

23. Why did the Wrights have to move again soon after they got to West Helena?
    A. They couldn't pay the rent and had to find a less expensive place.
    B. The house was so dirty and dilapidated they couldn't stand it.
    C. They had an argument with the landlady, and she evicted them.
    D. The house burned down.

24. What happened to Aunt Maggie and "uncle?"
    A. They got married because she was pregnant.
    B. They were forced to leave because white men were looking for "uncle."
    C. "Uncle" got a good job and they moved to Detroit.
    D. They broke up because he beat her.

25. Richard was unable to sell Betsy to a white woman because of his anxieties. A week later the dog was run over in his own neighborhood, leaving him without dog or money. What literary device is this?
    A. Foreshadowing
    B. Irony
    C. Satire
    D. Metamorphosis

Black Boy-Multiple Choice Study/Quiz Questions Page 6

<u>Chapter 3-4</u>

26. What happened to Richard after his mother had a stroke?
    A. He was sent to an orphanage.
    B. He went to Chicago.
    C. He moved in with his Uncle Clark and Aunt Jody.
    D. He stayed with Granny.

27. What forced Richard to ask to leave Greenwood?
    A. He was afraid of his aunt because she was constantly threatening to beat him. She was also starting to force him to steal things at the local grocery store. He knew he had to get away from her.
    B. He couldn't learn in school. The principal refused to promote him to the next grade, and he was too embarrassed to stay in a class where he was the oldest.
    C. He got in trouble with the neighborhood gang and was afraid he would be killed.
    D. He found out that a boy had died in the bed in which he slept. He didn't want to sleep in the bed and wasn't permitted to sleep anywhere else. He became exhausted and asked to be returned to his mother.

28.-30. Richard's mothers illness had several effects on him. Circle A for the statements about her illness that are true or circle B for the statements that are false.

28. His mother's suffering grew in his mind as a symbol of meaningless pain, helplessness, and hunger.
    A. True
    B. False

29. Her life had no effect on the emotional tone of his life.
    A. True
    B. False

30. Richard developed a somberness of spirit that never left him.
    A. True
    B. False.

31. Who was Granny's ally in trying to make Richard get religion?
    A. It was the minister's son.
    B. It was Richard's brother.
    C. It was Aunt Addie.
    D. It was the school principal.

Black Boy-Multiple Choice Study/Quiz Questions Page 7

32. Why did Addie beat Richard?
    A. He had beaten up another boy in the class.
    B. She had a preconceived notion that he was a bad boy and didn't believe him when he was defending himself.
    C. She thought he had cheated on a test because he got the highest grade in the class.
    D. She was angry at Richard's mother and was taking it out on him.

33. What was Richard's reaction?
    A. He refused to be beaten unjustly and defended himself with a knife.
    B. He apologized to her to keep peace in the family.
    C. He cried in front of the rest of the class to get their sympathy.
    D. He took the punishment and acted as though he didn't care because he knew that would bother her even more.

34. How did Granny get embarrassed in church?
    A. Richard sang the wrong words to the hymns, very loudly and out of tune.
    B. Someone commented about Richard's shabby appearance, and Granny overheard it.
    C. She fell asleep and was snoring. Richard thought it was funny and didn't try to wake her up.
    D. She misunderstood something he said and told the preacher Richard had seen an angel. Richard scolded Granny for her error in front of the other church members.

35. Why did Richard write his first story?
    A. He was bored with prayer, and writing gave him an escape from his oppressive life.
    B. There was a contest at school, and he wanted to win the $10 prize.
    C. He was trying to impress a girl in his class who was very studious.
    D. He did it to defy Granny.

Black Boy-Multiple Choice Study/Quiz Questions Page 8

Chapters 5-6

36. How did Richard's family react to his sixth grade promotion?
    A. They were happy and had a party.
    B. They didn't believe a boy as bad as he was could do it.
    C. They thanked Aunt Addie because they thought she had promoted him even though he didn't deserve it.
    D. They ignored it. No one really cared what happened to him.

37. Why did Richard sell the anti-Negro newspapers?
    A. His grandmother forced him to do it.
    B. It was his misguided form of social protest.
    C. He didn't know the content; he just wanted to read the magazine section of stories and to make a little money.
    D. Some white boys he knew had threatened to hurt his mother and grandmother if he didn't sell the papers.

38. Why did Addie say she would kill Richard?
    A. She found out he was organizing the other students against her.
    B. She blamed Richard for Granny's accident.
    C. There was not enough money for food, and she was desperate. She reasoned that it would be one less mouth to feed.
    D. She was obsessed with the thought that he was evil and should be destroyed.

39. Who was brother Manse?
    A. He was an assistant deacon at the church.
    B. He was Richard's new teacher.
    C. He was another friend who came to live with Richard.
    D. He was Richard's next door neighbor who gave him the job of reading and writing for him in his insurance work.

40. What did Richard gain from his association with Brother Manse?
    A. He learned the insurance business.
    B. He made a lot of money that enabled him to move out of his grandmother's house.
    C. He gained thirty pounds because Brother Manse was always feeding him.
    D. He gained a new outlook on life and a little self-respect.

41. How did Addie and Granny react to Grandpa's death?
    A. They were very emotional, crying and mourning loudly.
    B. They were cold and unemotional.
    C. They stopped talking altogether.
    D. They cried but only when they were alone.

Black Boy-Multiple Choice Study/Quiz Questions Page 9

42. What was Richard's mother's reaction to his defiance of Granny and Addie and their consequent consent to his working.
    A. She was indifferent.
    B. She smiled and kissed him.
    C. She told him he was a fool.
    D. She insisted that he promise to give her all of his savings.

43. Why didn't Richard want to work for the white woman who gave him moldy molasses?
    A. She didn't pay him enough.
    B. She had assaulted his ego.
    C. The work was boring and not challenging enough.
    D. The work hours interfered with his schooling.

44. Why did Richard begin to attend Sunday school?
    A. The minister offered him a part-time job, but he could only have it if he attended Sunday School.
    B. He went because there was a free lunch every Sunday and he was always hungry.
    C. He went to talk and be with his friends.
    D. He was becoming curious about religion.

45. Why did Richard finally consent to being baptized into the church?
    A. He did it out of love for his mother, so she wouldn't be humiliated.
    B. His friends were putting pressure on him to join.
    C. He honestly believed he had "gotten the faith."
    D. He was too run down and tired to argue any more.

46. Why did Richard threaten to cut his Uncle Tom with razors?
    A. He found out that Uncle Tom was stealing food from the pantry at night after everyone else had gone to bed.
    B. Uncle Tom was disrespectful to Richard's mother, and Richard couldn't stand it.
    C. Richard wanted to be the man of the house, so he thought he had to show Uncle Tom and the others how tough he could be.
    D. Uncle Tom had, from Richard's viewpoint, unjustly threatened to beat him, and Richard would not allow that to happen.

Black Boy-Multiple Choice Study/Quiz Questions Page 10

Chapters 7-8

47. What was The Voodoo of Hell's Half Acre?
    A. It was the first movie that Richard ever saw.
    B. It was the first story that Richard wrote for publication.
    C. It was a book of chants and spells that he secretly read at the library. It was in the adult section, and the librarian wouldn't let him check it out. He thought he could find a chant to reverse his mother's illness.
    D. It was a sermon preached by a guest minister at the church. It was the first speech on racism that Richard had ever heard.

48. Richard said one particular place symbolized "...all that I had not felt and seen; it had no relation whatever to what actually existed. Yet, by imagining a place where everything was possible, I kept hope alive in me." What was this place?
    A. It was the white area of the city.
    B. It was heaven.
    C. It was the North.
    D. It was the world he was creating in his writing.

49. What effect did the death of Ned's brother, Bob, have on Richard?
    A. It had no effect.
    B. He felt that the death penalty was waiting for him if he made a false move, and he wondered whether to make any moves.
    C. It angered him and made him more rebellious and defiant.
    D. He became very depressed, wouldn't eat, and had nightmares for a few weeks.

50. Why did Richard refuse to deliver the pre-written graduation speech?
    A. He felt that his speech should be his own instead of a piece prepared by others for social or political reasons.
    B. He was ashamed to admit he couldn't read it.
    C. He didn't want to be set apart from the other boys.
    D. It was his form of protest, to let the school officials know that he thought he had received an inadequate education.

Black Boy-Multiple Choice Study/Quiz Questions Page 11

Chapter 9-11
51-53 Three incidents left an impression on Richard during his time working at the clothing store.

51. He saw a black woman raped by his bosses, and the white policemen sided with the white bosses.
    A. Yes, this was one of the events.
    B. No, this was not one of the events.

52. The white boys beat him up for looking at a white person the street.
    A. Yes, this was one of the events.
    B. No, this was not one of the events.

53. He was chased out of the neighborhood by dogs released by a few of the inhabitants.
    A. Yes, this was one of the events.
    B. No, this was not one of the events.

54. What advice did Griggs give Richard?
    A. "When you're in front of white people, think before you act, think before you speak. Your way of doing this is all right among our people, but not for white people. They won't stand for it."
    B. "Get all the money and information you can without making yourself obvious. Then get out of the way."
    C. "Never stop rebelling. We have to fight the white man until we defeat him or die trying."
    D. "Give yourself to God. His love will get you through this life better than anything else."

55. Why did Richard quit working at the optical company?
    A. A competitor offered him a better job.
    B. The smells from the chemicals were making him sick.
    C. Two white employees ganged up on him and threatened to kill him if he told the boss about their abuse of him.
    D. He was beginning to think he could make a successful career of writing, and he wanted to have more time to write.

56. Who was the good-hearted white man from the North who tried to help Richard?
    A. It was Mr. Reynolds.
    B. It was Mr. Harrison.
    C. It was Mr. Crane.
    D. It was Mr. Bibbs.

Black Boy-Multiple Choice Study/Quiz Questions Page 12

57. How did Richard get enough money to go North?
    A. He didn't. He hid inside a boxcar and rode for free.
    B. He took a job at a movie house and took part in a scheme which skimmed money from ticket sales.
    C. He robbed a grocery store.
    D. He picked pockets in a few of the black neighborhoods.

58. Why did Richard resort to crime?
    A. He really wanted to get arrested. He had heard that in jail he would have a warm place to live, clean clothes, and regular meals. This was appealing to him.
    B. He found out he liked the thrill of it. It was the only part of his existence where he really felt alive.
    C. He was under pressure from his family and friends to do so.
    D. He could not honestly earn enough to live and save money. He felt as though he had no choice.

59. Who was Mrs. Moss?
    A. She was a woman he met on the train. She shared her lunch with him.
    B. She was a storekeeper who told him where he might be able to find a job.
    C. She was a woman who had rooms for rent. Richard stayed with her.
    D. She was a friend of his grandmother's who gave him some money.

60. Who was Bess?
    A. She was a cousin he first met when he moved to Memphis. She was a good listener and helped him sort things out.
    B. She was Mrs. Moss's daughter.
    C. She was a girl he met at work. He thought he was falling in love with her.
    D. She was the local librarian. She recommended books for him to read, and then the two discussed them.

61. What plans did Mrs. Moss have for Richard?
    A. She wanted him to fix up her house.
    B. She wanted him to become the landlord so she could move to another building.
    C. She thought he had great potential as a preacher. She wanted to help him set up a church.
    D. She wanted him to marry her daughter.

Black Boy-Multiple Choice Study/Quiz Questions Page 13

62. There were many reasons that Richard refused Bess. Which of these was not one of the reasons?
    A. He was afraid his mother would not approve.
    B. He was overwhelmed by her offer.
    C. He didn't love her.
    D. He felt he would be trapped and never get to the North.

Black Boy-Multiple Choice Study/Quiz Questions Page 14

Chapters 12-14

63. Identify Shorty.
    A. He was another young black writer whom Richard met. They critiqued each other's manuscripts.
    B. He was a boy Richard met on the street. He knew the city very well and was adept at stealing from local merchants.
    C. He was the elevator operator in the building where Richard worked. He would do almost anything for money.
    D. He was the boss's son. He took a personal interest in Richard.

64. Why did Richard fight Harrison?
    A. He was afraid of what the white men would do to him if he refused.
    B. The two of them agreed to only pretend to hurt each other.
    C. He really hated Harrison and was glad to get the chance to fight him.
    D. He desperately needed the money that the white men promised to give him.

65. What was the result of the fight?
    A. It was broken up by the police and both boys were taken to jail.
    B. It was called off at the last minute because the boss found out about it and stopped it. The white men denied any involvement, so Richard and Harrison were both fired.
    C. They both enjoyed it so much they decided to hold more matches.
    D. They fought until they were exhausted, and Richard felt he had done something unclean.

66. What author/editor intrigued Richard?
    A. It was H.L. Mencken.
    B. It was Langston Hughes.
    C. It was William Randolph Hearst.
    D. It was Mark Twain.

67. How did Richard manage to get books from the library?
    A. He made arrangements with a Catholic white man at work, Mr. Falk, to pretend to be sent from Falk to get books from the library.
    B. He became friends with the cleaning woman. She sneaked the books out to him at night.
    C. He offered to work the library for free in return for the privilege of borrowing books.
    D. He started following the librarian home at night. He threatened to hurt her if she didn't bring him books. She complied.

Black Boy-Multiple Choice Study/Quiz Questions Page 15

68. What effect did the books have on Richard?
    A. They made him even angrier and more frustrated with his situation.
    B. They numbed him and kept him from thinking about reality.
    C. They gave him hope and educated him.
    D. They made him feel superior to the other blacks he knew, and then he felt very isolated. He stopped reading.

ANSWER KEY - MULTIPLE CHOICE STUDY/QUIZ QUESTIONS
Black Boy

CHAPTER 1	CHAPTER 2	CHAPTERS 3-4	CHAPTERS 5-6
1. C	17. B	26. C	36. B
2. A	18. B	27. D	37. C
3. B	19. A	28. A	38. B
4. D	20. C	29. B	39. D
5. A	21. A	30. A	40. A
6. C	22. D	31. C	41. B
7. B	23. C	32. B	42. B
8. A	24. B	33. A	43. B
9. D	25. B	34. D	44. C
10. A		35. A	45. A
11. B			46. D
12. B			
13. D			
14. C			
15. C			
16. A			

CHAPTERS 7-8	CHAPTERS 9-11	CHAPTERS 12-14
47. B	51. A	63. C
48. C	52. B	64. B
49. B	53. B	65. D
50. A	54. A	66. A
	55. C	67. A
	56. C	68. C
	57. B	
	58. D	
	59. C	
	60. B	
	61. D	
	62. A	

PREREADING VOCABULARY
WORKSHEETS

VOCABULARY - *Black Boy*

<u>Chapter 1</u> Part I: Using Prior Knowledge and Contextual Clues

Below are the sentences in which the vocabulary words appear in the text. Read the sentence. Use any clues you can find in the sentence combined with your prior knowledge, and write what you think the underlined words mean in the space provided.

1. I <u>yearned</u> to become invisible, to stop living.

2. Then I saw her taut face <u>peering</u> under the edge of the house.

3. There were the echoes of <u>nostalgia</u> I heard in the crying strings of wild geese winging south against a bleak, autumn sky.

4. As evening drew near, <u>anxiety</u> filled me and I was afraid to go into an empty room alone.

5. The boys scattered, yelling, nursing their heads, staring at me in utter disbelief. They had never seen such <u>frenzy</u>.

6. She beat me; then she prayed and wept over me, <u>imploring</u> me to be good, telling me that she had to work.

7. ...I would question her so <u>relentlessly</u> about what I had heard in the streets that she refused to talk to me.

8. ...my mother's <u>ardently</u> religious disposition dominated the household and I was often taken to Sunday school...

9. The children were silent, hostile, <u>vindictive</u>, continuously complaining of hunger.

10. ...their faces...would surge up in my imagination so <u>vivid</u> and strong that I felt I could reach out and touch it..

Vocabulary Worksheet *Black Boy* Chapter 1 Continued

Part II: Determining the Meaning -- Match the vocabulary words to their definitions.

_____ 1. yearned A. Making an earnest appeal
_____ 2. peering B. Heard, seen or felt as if real
_____ 3. nostalgia C. Had a strong, often melancholy desire
_____ 4. anxiety D. Steadily; persistently
_____ 5. frenzy E. Looking intently, searchingly, or with difficulty
_____ 6. imploring F. A state of violent or wild excitement
_____ 7. relentlessly G. Revengeful
_____ 8. ardently H. A bittersweet longing for things of the past
_____ 9. vindictive I. Characterized by strong enthusiasm or devotion
_____ 10. vivid J. A state of uneasiness and apprehension

Vocabulary *Black Boy* Chapter 2

Part I: Using Prior Knowledge and Contextual Clues

Below are the sentences in which the vocabulary words appear in the text. Read the sentence. Use any clues you can find in the sentence combined with your prior knowledge, and write what you think the underlined words mean in the space provided.

1. I asked myself if these human qualities were not fostered, won, struggled and suffered for, preserved in <u>ritual</u> from one generation to another.

2. Enchanted and <u>enthralled</u>, I stopped her constantly to ask for details.

3. ...I would buy all the novels there were and read them to feed that thirst for violence that was in me, for <u>intrigue</u>, for plotting, for secrecy, for bloody murders.

4. They read my insistence as mere <u>obstinacy</u>, as foolishness, something that would quickly pass; and they had no notion how desperately serious the tale had made me.

5. He was under the <u>delusion</u> that the war between the states would be resumed.

6. There was the <u>aura</u> of limitless freedom distilled from the rolling sweep of tall green grass swaying and glinting in the wind and sun.

7. So, <u>surreptitiously</u>, I took some of the biscuits from the platter and slipped them into my pocket, not to eat, but to keep as a bulwark against any possible attack of hunger.

8. All of us black people who lived in the neighborhood hated Jews, not because they <u>exploited</u> us, but because we had been taught at home and in Sunday school that Jews were "Christ killers."

9. To hold an attitude of <u>antagonism</u> or distrust toward Jews was bred in us from childhood...

10. I resolved that I would <u>emulate</u> the black woman if I were faced with a white mob...

Vocabulary Worksheet *Black Boy* Chapter 2 Continued

Part II: Determining the Meaning -- Match the vocabulary words to their definitions.

_____ 1. ritual
_____ 2. enthralled
_____ 3. intrigue
_____ 4. obstinacy
_____ 5. delusion
_____ 6. aura
_____ 7. surreptitiously
_____ 8. exploited
_____ 9. antagonism
_____ 10. emulate

A. Imitate
B. Atmosphere
C. Hostility that results in active resistance or opposition
D. Ceremony
E. Spellbound; captivated
F. A false belief or opinion
G. Stubbornness
H. A secret or underhanded scheme
I. Stealthily
J. A false belief or opinion

Vocabulary *Black Boy* Chapter 3

Part I: Using Prior Knowledge and Contextual Clues
   Below are the sentences in which the vocabulary words appear in the text. Read the sentence. Use any clues you can find in the sentence combined with your prior knowledge, and write what you think the underlined words mean in the space provided.

1. ...I would stumble upon one or more of the gang loitering at a corner, standing in a field, or sitting upon the steps of somebody's house.

2. "How come?" Feigned innocence.

3. I was glad that my mother was not dead, but there was the fact that she would be sick for a long time, perhaps for the balance of her life. I became morose.

4. I had been waiting for a fiat, and now a choice lay before me.

5. I had always felt a certain warmth with my mother, even when we lived in squalor; but I felt none here.

6. ...a group of boys sauntered up to me, looked at me from my head to my feet....

7. I went to Uncle Clark, knowing that he had incurred expense in bringing me here...

8. ...I had a conception of life that no experience would ever erase, a predilection for what was real that no argument could ever gainsay...

Part II: Determining the Meaning -- Match the vocabulary words to their definitions.
   _____1. loitering   A. Gave a false appearance of; pretended
   _____2. feigned   B. Acquired
   _____3. morose   C. Preference
   _____4. fiat   D. Gloomy
   _____5. squalor   E. Standing idly about; lingering with no purpose
   _____6. sauntered   F. A filthy and wretched condition
   _____7. incurred   G. An order or authorization
   _____8. predilection   H. Strolled

Vocabulary *Black Boy* Chapter 4

Part I: Using Prior Knowledge and Contextual Clues
Below are the sentences in which the vocabulary words appear in the text. Read the sentence. Use any clues you can find in the sentence combined with your prior knowledge, and write what you think the underlined words mean in the space provided.

1. These boys and girls were will-less, their speech flat, their gestures vague, their personalities devoid of anger, hope, laughter, enthusiasm, passion, or despair.

2. ...I had taken punishment that was not mine to protect the solidarity of the gang...

3. "Stand still, boy!" she blazed, her face livid with fury, her body trembling.

4. And it was presumed that I prayed before I got into bed at night.

5. ...she had come to the conclusion that my lost soul was more valuable than petty pride.

6. "I simple can't feel religion," I told him in lieu of telling him that I did not think I had the kind of soul he though I had.

7. During our talk I made a hypothetical statement that summed up my attitude toward God...

8. Frightened and baffled, he left me.

9. The boy had no doubt conveyed to her my words of blasphemy...

10. I must have looked dubious, for he said: "Really, I do."

Vocabulary Worksheet *Black Boy* Chapter 4 Continued

Part II: Determining the Meaning -- Match the vocabulary words to their definitions.

_____ 1. devoid   A. Trivial
_____ 2. solidarity   B. Discolored; showing extreme anger
_____ 3. livid   C. Doubtful
_____ 4. presume   D. Completely lacking or empty
_____ 5. petty   E. In place of
_____ 6. lieu   F. A union of interests, or purposes among group members
_____ 7. hypothetical   G. Take for granted as being true
_____ 8. baffled   H. To speak of God in an irreverent manner
_____ 9. blasphemy   I. Suppositional
_____10. dubious   J. Puzzled; confused

Vocabulary *Black Boy* Chapters 5-6

Part I: Using Prior Knowledge and Contextual Clues

Below are the sentences in which the vocabulary words appear in the text. Read the sentence. Use any clues you can find in the sentence combined with your prior knowledge, and write what you think the underlined words mean in the space provided.

1. From urgent solicitude they dropped to coldness and hostility.

2. With pencil and tablet, I walked nonchalantly into the schoolyard, wearing a cheap, brand-new straw hat.

3. When I returned home at night, I would go to my room and lock the door and revel in outlandish exploits of outlandish men in faraway, outlandish cities.

4. In the man's red-dotted tie was a dazzling horseshoe stickpin, glaring conspicuously.

5. As summer waned I obtained a strange job.

6. A tall, dour white woman talked to me.

7. As they hurled invectives, they barely looked at each other.

8. But the job had its boon.

9. "Why, you impudent black rascal!" he thundered.

Vocabulary Worksheet *Black Boy* Chapters 5-6 Continued

Part II: Determining the Meaning -- Match the vocabulary words to their definitions.

_____ 1. solicitude   A. To take great pleasure or delight
_____ 2. nonchalantly   B. Approached an end
_____ 3. revel   C. A benefit
_____ 4. conspicuously   D. Seeming to be coolly unconcerned or indifferent
_____ 5. waned   E. Obviously
_____ 6. dour   F. Abusive language
_____ 7. invectives   G. Care or concern as for the well being of another
_____ 8. boon   H. Offensively bold
_____ 9. impudent   I. Silently ill-humored or sternly obstinate

Vocabulary *Black Boy* Chapters 7-8

Part I: Using Prior Knowledge and Contextual Clues
Below are the sentences in which the vocabulary words appear in the text. Read the sentence. Use any clues you can find in the sentence combined with your prior knowledge, and write what you think the underlined words mean in the space provided.

1. It was <u>inconceivable</u> to me that one should surrender to what seemed wrong...

2. It was crudely atmospheric, emotional <u>intuitively</u> psychological, and stemmed from pure feeling.

3. Uncle Tom, though surprised, was highly critical and <u>contemptuous</u>.

4. Had I been articulate about my ultimate <u>aspirations</u>, no doubt someone would have told me what I was bargaining for...

5. What I had heard altered the look of the world, <u>induced</u> in me a temporary paralysis of will and impulse.

6. ...my sense of isolation became doubly <u>acute</u>.

7. I was poised for flight, but I was waiting for some event, some word, some act, some circumstances to furnish the <u>impetus</u>.

8. He laughed confidently, <u>indulgently</u>.

Part II: Determining the Meaning -- Match the vocabulary words to their definitions.
_____ 1. inconceivable   A. Caused
_____ 2. intuitively   B. Sharp or severe; intense
_____ 3. contemptuous   C. Without the use of rational reasoning; instinctively
_____ 4. aspirations   D. An impelling force
_____ 5. induced   E. Leniently; patiently
_____ 6. acute   F. Impossible to comprehend or fully grasp
_____ 7. impetus   G. Ambitions
_____ 8. indulgently   H. Scornful

Vocabulary *Black Boy* Chapters 9-11

Part I: Using Prior Knowledge and Contextual Clues
Below are the sentences in which the vocabulary words appear in the text. Read the sentence. Use any clues you can find in the sentence combined with your prior knowledge, and write what you think the underlined words mean in the space provided.

1. They seemed dissatisfied when they could find nothing <u>incriminating</u>.

2. I would remember to <u>dissemble</u> for short periods, then I would forget and act straight and human again, not with the desire to harm anybody, but merely forgetting the artificial status of race and class.

3. I even pitched my voice to a low plane, trying to rob it of any suggestion or <u>overtone</u> of aggressiveness.

4. I worked through the days and tried to hide my resentment under a nervous, <u>cryptic</u> smile.

5. I looked at the white faces of Pease and Reynolds; I imagined their <u>waylaying</u> me, killing me.

6. I waited and my <u>roused</u> senses grew slowly calm.

7. They did not seem to be individual men, but part of a huge, <u>implacable</u>, elemental design toward which hate was futile.

8. I cleaned acres of glass shelving, changing my tempo now to work faster, holding every <u>nuance</u> of reality within the focus of my consciousness.

9. My body jerked <u>taut</u> and I stared at him.

Vocabulary Worksheet *Black Boy* Chapters 9-11 Continued

Part II: Determining the Meaning -- Match the vocabulary words to their definitions.

_____ 1. incriminating   A. Tending to conceal or camouflage
_____ 2. dissemble   B. Impossible to please or satisfy
_____ 3. overtone   C. An ulterior meaning or quality; an implication or hint
_____ 4. cryptic   D. Tight; tense
_____ 5. waylaying   E. Excited as to anger or action; stirred up
_____ 6. roused   F. To cause to appear guilty of a crime or fault
_____ 7. implacable   G. Subtle or slight degree of difference
_____ 8. nuance   H. To disguise one's real nature, motives or feelings
_____ 9. taut   I. Ambushing; intercepting someone unexpectedly

Vocabulary *Black Boy* Chapters 9-11 Page 2

10. I could not make subservience an automatic part of my behavior.

11. The girl twisted out of his reach, tossed her head saucily, and went down the hallway.

12. The mere idea of stealing had become repugnant.

13. More than once I had been called a "dumb nigger" by black boys who discovered that I had not availed myself of a chance to snatch some petty piece of white property that had been carelessly left within my reach.

14. My larcenous aims were modest.

15. I gave him a pledge of my honesty, feeling absolutely no qualms about what I intended to do.

16. He grew violently angry and I quickly consented to stay, fearing that someone might turn me in for revenge, or to get me out of the way so that another and more pliable boy could have my place.

Part II: Determining the Meaning -- Match the vocabulary words to their definitions.

_____	10. subservience	A. Disrespectfully
_____	11. saucily	B. Made use of
_____	12. repugnant	C. Characterized by theft
_____	13. availed	D. Easily influenced or persuaded
_____	14. larcenous	E. Uneasy feeling about the rightness of an action
_____	15. qualms	F. Being subordinate; of a lesser position
_____	16. pliable	G. Offensive or repulsive

Vocabulary *Black Boy* Chapters 12-14

Part I: Using Prior Knowledge and Contextual Clues

Below are the sentences in which the vocabulary words appear in the text. Read the sentence. Use any clues you can find in the sentence combined with your prior knowledge, and write what you think the underlined words mean in the space provided.

1.-2. It was fairly easy to contemplate the race issue in the shop without reaching those heights of fear that devastated me.

3. I now had more money than I had ever had before, and I began patronizing secondhand bookstores, buying magazines and books.

4. But in the presence of whites he would play the role of a clown of the most debased and degraded type.

5-6. Hence, our daily lives were so bound up with trivial objectives that to capitulate when challenged was tantamount to surrendering to the right to life itself.

7. (There are some elusive, profound, recondite things that men find hard to say to other men; but with the Negro it is the little things of life that become hard to say, for these tiny items shape his destiny.

8. We agreed to ignore any further provocations.

9. The article was a furious denunciation of Mencken, concluding with one, hot, short sentence: Mencken is a fool.

10. His position was not much better than mine and I knew that he was uneasy and insecure; he had always treated me in an offhand, bantering way that barely concealed his contempt.

Vocabulary Worksheet *Black Boy* Chapters 12-14 Continued

Part II: Determining the Meaning -- Match the vocabulary words to their definitions

_____ 1. Contemplate   A. Public condemnation or censure
_____ 2. devastated   B. Not easily understood
_____ 3. patronizing   C. Lowered in character, quality or value
_____ 4. debased   D. Speaking in a playful or teasing way
_____ 5. capitulate   E. Going to as a customer
_____ 6. tantamount   F. Destroyed
_____ 7. recondite   G. Something that incites or is intended to cause trouble
_____ 8. provocations   H. Think about
_____ 9. denunciation   I. Equivalent in effect or value
_____10. bantering   J. Surrender; give up

ANSWER KEY - VOCABULARY
Black Boy

Chapter 1
1. C
2. E
3. H
4. J
5. F
6. A
7. D
8. I
9. G
10. B

Chapter 2
1. D
2. E
3. H
4. G
5. F
6. B
7. I
8. J
9. C
10. A

Chapters 3
1. E
2. A
3. D
4. G
5. F
6. H
7. B
8. C

Chapter 4
1. D
2. F
3. B
4. G
5. A
6. E
7. I
8. J
9. H
10. C

Chapters 5-6
1. G
2. D
3. A
4. E
5. B
6. I
7. F
8. C
9. H

Chapters 7-8
1. F
2. C
3. H
4. G
5. A
6. B
7. D
8. E

Chapters 9-11
1. F
2. H
3. C
4. A
5. I
6. E
7. B
8. G
9. D
10. F
11. A
12. G
13. B
14. C
15. E
16. D

Chapters 12-14
1. H
2. F
3. E
4. C
5. J
6. I
7. B
8. G
9. A
10. D

DAILY LESSONS

LESSON ONE

Objectives
1. To introduce the *Black Boy* unit.
2. To distribute books and other related materials
3. To preview the study questions for Book One
4. To familiarize students with the vocabulary for Book One

NOTE: Prior to this lesson, tell students to bring in a photo of themselves. You also need a sheet of construction paper for each student. Prepare a bulletin board with background paper and a title: AU-TO-BI-OG-RA-PHY n., pl. -phies. THE STORY OF A PERSON'S LIFE WRITTEN BY HIMSELF.

Activity #1

Have students write short autobiographies of themselves (1-2 paragraphs). They should include when and where they were born, a little about their parent(s), and the main events that have happened in their lives from the time they were born to the present time.

Students should paste, tape, or staple their pictures onto the top center of the construction paper and then write a "good copy" of their autobiographies under the pictures.

Have students post their autobiographical sketches on a bulletin board or vacant wall in your classroom. If you have no classroom, or if you prefer, you could collect all of the autobiographical sketches, compile them into a booklet, and print (photocopy) a copy of the booklet for everyone in your class to have.

TRANSITION: Explain that the book you are about to read, *Black Boy* by Richard Wright, is autobiographical in nature.

Activity #2

Distribute the materials students will use in this unit. Explain in detail how students are to use these materials.

<u>Study Guides</u> Students should read the study guide questions for each reading assignment prior to beginning the reading assignment to get a feeling for what events and ideas are important in the section they are about to read. After reading the section, students will (as a class or individually) answer the questions to review the important events and ideas from that section of the book. Students should keep the study guides as study materials for the unit test.

<u>Vocabulary</u> Prior to reading a reading assignment, students will do vocabulary work related to the section of the book they are about to read. Following the completion of the reading of the book, there will be a vocabulary review of all the words used in the vocabulary assignments. Students should keep their vocabulary work as study materials for the unit test.

<u>Reading Assignment Sheet</u> You need to fill in the reading assignment sheet to let students know by when their reading has to be completed. You can either write the assignment sheet up on a side blackboard or bulletin board and leave it there for students to see each day, or you can "ditto" copies for each student to have. In either case, you should advise students to become very familiar with the reading assignments so they know what is expected of them.

<u>Extra Activities Center</u> The Extra Activities section of this unit contains suggestions for an extra library of related books and articles in your classroom as well as crossword and word search puzzles. Make an extra activities center in your room where you will keep these materials for students to use. (Bring the books and articles in from the library and keep several copies of the puzzles on hand.) Explain to students that these materials are available for students to use when they finish reading assignments or other class work early.

<u>Nonfiction Assignment Sheet</u> Explain to students that they each are to read at least one non-fiction piece from the in-class library at some time during the unit. Students will fill out a nonfiction assignment sheet after completing the reading to help you evaluate their reading experiences and to help the students think about and evaluate their own reading experiences.

<u>Books</u> Each school has its own rules and regulations regarding student use of school books. Advise students of the procedures that are normal for your school.

<u>Activity #3</u>
Preview the study questions and have students do the vocabulary work for Chapter 1 of *Black Boy*. If students do not finish this assignment during this class period, they should complete it prior to the next class meeting.

NONFICTION ASSIGNMENT SHEET
(To be completed after reading the required nonfiction article)

Name _____ Date _____

Title of Nonfiction Read _____

Written By _____ Publication Date _____

I. Factual Summary: Write a short summary of the piece you read.

II. Vocabulary
    1. With which vocabulary words in the piece did you encounter some degree of difficulty?

    2. How did you resolve your lack of understanding with these words?

III. Interpretation: What was the main point the author wanted you to get from reading his work?

IV. Criticism
    1. With which points of the piece did you agree or find easy to accept? Why?

    2. With which points of the piece did you disagree or find difficult to believe? Why?

V. Personal Response: What do you think about this piece? OR How does this piece influence your ideas?

LESSON TWO

Objectives
1. To read Book One
2. To give students the opportunity to practice oral reading
3. To give the teacher the opportunity to evaluate students' reading skills
4. To preview the study questions and vocabulary for Chapter 2

Activity #1
Have students read Chapter 1 of *Black Boy* aloud in class. You probably know the best way to get readers with your class; pick students at random, ask for volunteers, or use whatever method works best for your group. If you have not yet completed an oral reading evaluation for your students this marking period, this would be a good opportunity to do so. A form is included with this unit for your convenience.

Activity #2
Tell students that they should complete reading Chapter 1 and do the prereading work for Chapter 2 prior to your next class meeting. (Give students a day/date.) (The "prereading work" is to preview the study questions and to do the prereading vocabulary worksheet(s).

LESSON THREE

Objectives
1. To review the main events and ideas from Chapter 1
2. To preview the study questions for Chapter 3
3. To familiarize students with the vocabulary in Chapter 3
4. To read Chapter 2

Activity #1
Give students a few minutes to formulate answers for the study guide questions for Chapter 1 and then discuss the answers to the questions in detail. Write the answers on the board or overhead transparency so students can have the correct answers for study purposes. NOTE: It is a good practice in public speaking and leadership skills for individual students to take charge of leading the discussions of the study questions. Perhaps a different student could go to the front of the class and lead the discussion each day that the study questions are discussed during this unit. Of course, the teacher should guide the discussion when appropriate and be sure to fill in any gaps the students leave.

Activity #2
Have students read Chapter 2 of *Black Boy* out loud in class. If you are doing the oral reading evaluations, have students continue reading orally. If you are not doing the oral reading evaluations, have students get together in pairs and take turns reading to each other. Tell students that prior to your next class period they should have completed reading Chapter 2 and should have completed the prereading work for Chapter 3.

ORAL READING EVALUATION - *Black Boy*

Name _____ Class____ Date _____

SKILL	EXCELLENT	GOOD	AVERAGE	FAIR	POOR
Fluency	5	4	3	2	1
Clarity	5	4	3	2	1
Audibility	5	4	3	2	1
Pronunciation	5	4	3	2	1
_____	5	4	3	2	1
_____	5	4	3	2	1

Total _____ Grade _____

Comments:

LESSON FOUR

Objectives
1. To review the main events and ideas from Chapter 2
2. To preview the study questions for Chapter 4
3. To familiarize students with the vocabulary in Chapter 4
4. To read Chapter 3

Activity #1
Give students a few minutes to formulate answers for the study guide questions for Chapter 2 and then discuss the answers to the questions in detail. Write the answers on the board or overhead transparency so students can have the correct answers for study purposes.

Activity #2
Have students read Chapter 3 of *Black Boy* out loud in class. If you are doing the oral reading evaluations, continue with those and have students read orally. If you are not doing the evaluations or have completed them, have students read silently during this class period.

Activity #3
Tell students that prior to your next class period they should have completed reading Chapter 3 and should have completed the prereading and reading work for Chapter 4.

LESSON FIVE

Objectives
1. To review the main ideas and events from Chapter 3
2. To preview and read chapters 5-6
3. To give students the opportunity to express their personal opinions in writing
4. To give the teacher the opportunity to evaluate students' writing skills

Activity #1
Give students a few minutes to formulate answers to the study questions. Discuss the answers to the questions in detail. Write the answers on the board for students to copy for study use.

Activity #2
Tell students that prior to your next class meeting they should have completed the prereading and reading work for chapters 5-6. If students complete the writing assignment (Activity #3) early, they may begin working on this assignment.

Activity #3
Distribute Writing Assignment #1. Discuss the directions in detail and give students ample time to complete the assignment.

WRITING ASSIGNMENT #1 - *Black Boy*

PROMPT

Through the novel, *Black Boy*, Richard Wright not only gives a portrait of his own life but also gives us a vivid picture of what it meant to grow up as a black boy in the South after the Civil War but prior to the Civil Rights Movement. Regardless of the skin color, readers of this book are exposed to a powerful, moving story of a young boy's struggle to find and maintain his own individuality in a world seemingly set to cast and keep him in a stereotypical role. We know that Richard grew up, moved North, *did* maintain his individuality, and became a respected American writer. He continued to be dissatisfied with his life in the United States, though, and moved his residence to Europe.

How would Richard Wright feel about living in the United States today? What do you think he would write in a novel called *Black Boy* about a black boy growing up in the United States *today*? Your assignment is to write a composition in which you answer that question.

PREWRITING

Your first step is to stop and think. Brainstorm a list of ideas and impressions you have as an immediate response to the question. Jot them down. Now think a little longer and a little deeper. What are your second thoughts about the things you have written down and second responses to the question? Jot them down.

Look at what you have written. What things are the most important to characterize life for a black boy today? Place a star next to them. What are all the other things you have written? Choose a few of those items that you think would be important points in a present-day *Black Boy* book. Put a dash next to them. Scratch out the phrases and ideas that would really not have a place in the book.

Next to each of the items on your list (the * or -- items), write down a few notes explaining what you mean and why you believe each would be included in the book.

DRAFTING

Write a paragraph in which you introduce the idea that if Richard Wright were writing *Black Boy* today, he would include . . . (insert your main points).

In the body of your composition, write one paragraph for each of the items on your list. Each paragraph should have a topic sentence and be filled out with explanations, examples, and reasons why you believe these things would be included in the book.

Write a concluding paragraph in which you give your final thoughts and bring your composition to a close.

Black Boy Writing Assignment #1 Continued

PROMPT

When you finish the rough draft of your paper, ask a student who sits near you to read it. After reading your rough draft, he/she should tell you what he/she liked best about your work, which parts were difficult to understand, and ways in which your work could be improved. Reread your paper considering your critic's comments and make the corrections you think are necessary..

PROOFREADING

Do a final proofreading of your paper double-checking your grammar, spelling, organization, and the clarity of your ideas.

LESSON SIX

Objectives
1. To introduce the project for this unit
2. To have students read the kinds of things Richard read, things that influenced his life
3. To expand students' knowledge of some of the most renowned authors of all time

NOTE: It will be a great help to your students if you would have Mencken's writings about these authors in your classroom. Check your school library and public library and gather as much Mencken as you can find as resources for your students' research. Especially try to get copies of *A Book of Prefaces* and *Prejudices*.

Also, tell students if you are making a requirement about how much of the authors' works they have to read. As you know, some authors wrote short sketches and tales while others wrote huge novels. Are your students required to read an entire work by the author or will excerpts be acceptable?

Fill in the Project Assignment Sheet, placing students' names next to the authors' names. Try to give the authors whose writing is more difficult to your higher level students. Give authors whose writing is easier to read to your lower level students.

Activity

Take students to the library/media center. Distribute the Project Assignment sheet. Discuss the directions in detail. Give students ample time to complete the assignment, telling them when the final projects will be due. This unit schedules them in lessons fourteen and fifteen.

LESSON SEVEN

Objectives
1. To review the main ideas and events from Chapters 4-6
2. To preview and read Chapters 7-8
3. To give students time to work on their project assignments

Activity #1

Give students a few minutes to formulate answers to the study questions for chapters 4-6. Discuss the answers in detail and write them on the board for students to copy for study use.

Activity #2

Tell students that prior to your next class meeting they should have done the prereading and reading work for chapters 7-8.

Activity #3

Give students this class period to work on their research projects. If students have completed their research work, they may use their class time to do Activity #2.

PROJECT ASSIGNMENT SHEET - *Black Boy*

PROMPT

In Chapter Thirteen, Richard reads Mencken's books and is shocked and amazed by what he reads. He wrote, "Occasionally I glanced up to reassure myself that I was alone in the room. Who were these men about whom Mencken was talking so passionately? Who was Anatole France? Joseph Conrad . . . Nietzsche, and scores of others? Were these men real? Did they exist or had they existed? And how did one pronounce their names?" The list of authors given on that passage of *Black Boy* are listed on the next page.

ASSIGNMENT

Each of you has been assigned one of these authors. Your assignment has five parts: read what H. L. Mencken wrote about your author, read biographical information about your author, read something written by your author, read a critical review about the author's work, and give an oral presentation to the class about your author and your research.

GETTING STARTED

While you are in the library/media center, find biographical information about your author, some of the things your author wrote, and a critical review of your author's work. In the biographical information, you will probably find titles of your author's major works. Take notes as you read, jotting down the most important facts/information you find. Fill out a Nonfiction Assignment Sheet for each article or work of nonfiction you read relating to this assignment.

Black Boy Project Assignment Continued

AUTHOR	ASSIGNED TO	AUTHOR	ASSIGNED TO
H. L. MENCKEN		IBSEN	
JOSEPH CONRAD		BALZAC	
SINCLAIR LEWIS		BERNARD SHAW	
SHERWOOD ANDERSON		DUMAS	
DOSTOEVSKI		POE	
GEORGE MOORE		THOMAS MANN	
GUSTAVE FLAUBERT		O. HENRY	
MAUPASSANT		DREISER	
TOLSTOY		H. G. WELLS	
FRANK HARRIS		GOGOL	
MARK TWAIN		T. S. ELIOT	
THOMAS HARDY		GIDE	
ARNOLD BENNETT		BAUDELAIRE	
STEPHEN CRANE		EDGAR LEE MASTERS	
ZOLA		STENDHAL	
NORRIS		TURGENEV	
GORKY		HUNEKER	
BERGSON		NIETZSCHE	

LESSON EIGHT

Objectives
1. To review the main ideas and events from chapters 7-8
2. To give students the opportunity to practice writing to inform
3. To give the teacher the opportunity to evaluate students' writing skills
4. To help students organize their oral presentations
5. To preview and read chapters 9-11

Activity #1
Give students a few minutes to formulate answers to the study questions for chapters 7-8. Discuss the answers in detail and write them on the board for students to copy for study use.

Activity #2
Tell students that prior to your next class period they should have completed the prereading and reading work for chapters 9-11.

Activity #3
Distribute Writing Assignment #2. Discuss the directions in detail and give students ample time to complete the assignment. Be sure to tell students when their compositions will be due.

LESSON NINE

Objectives
1. To review the main ideas and events from chapters 9-11
2. To preview and read chapters 12-14

Activity #1
Give students a few minutes to formulate answers to the study questions for chapters 9-11. Discuss the answers in detail and write them on the board for students to copy for study use.

Activity #2
Give students about fifteen minutes to preview the study questions and do the prereading vocabulary work for chapters 12-14. After they complete this work, have them read chapters 12-14 either orally or silently.

WRITING ASSIGNMENT #2 - *Black Boy*

PROMPT

You have done (or are doing) your research for your oral presentation. When your research is finished, you need to organize your information and prepare your presentation. Your assignment is to write a composition in which you organize and state the basic information that will be in your presentation.

PREWRITING

You have done your research. Now you need to organize your information before you begin to write. You have information in four major categories: what Mencken said about your author, your author's biography, what critics have said about your author's work, and your opinions from your own reading of one of your author's writings. On four sheets of notebook paper, write the name of one of these categories at the top of each sheet (one category per sheet). On each paper, write down the main ideas for the category. For example, on your Mencken page, write down the main point(s) Mencken made about your author. On the critic's page, write down the main points the critic said about your author, etc. Next to each main point, jot down any examples, details, or explanations that support the point made.

DRAFTING

You may write this composition in a report style. First, write a paragraph of introduction in which you introduce your audience (your classmates) to your topic.

You will have four main headings in the body of your report: one for each of the categories in the PREWRITING heading above. Under each main heading, write one paragraph for each of the main points you jotted down for the category. Use a topic sentence to state your main point and then fill out the paragraph with examples, explanations, and/or details that support your statement.

Write a concluding paragraph in which you briefly summarize the information and bring your report to a close.

You will have one introductory paragraph, four main category headings with a few paragraphs for each heading, and a concluding paragraph in your report.

PROMPT

When you finish the rough draft of your report, ask a student who sits near you to read it. After reading your rough draft, he/she should tell you what he/she liked best about your work, which parts were difficult to understand, and ways in which your work could be improved. Reread your paper considering your critic's comments and make the corrections you think are necessary.

PROOFREADING

Do a final proofreading of your paper double-checking your grammar, spelling, organization, and the clarity of your ideas.

LESSON TEN

Objectives
1. To review the main ideas and events from Chapters 12-14
2. To discuss *Black Boy* on interpretive and critical levels

Activity #1
Give students a few minutes to formulate answers to the study questions for chapters 12-14. Discuss the answers and have students jot down the "correct" answers for study use.

Activity #2
Choose the questions from the Extra Discussion Questions/Writing Assignments which seem most appropriate for your students. A class discussion of these questions is most effective if students have been given the opportunity to formulate answers to the questions prior to the discussion. To this end, you may either have all the students formulate answers to all the questions, divide your class into groups, and assign one or more questions to each group, or you could assign one question to each student in your class. The option you choose will make a difference in the amount of class time needed for this activity.

After students have had ample time to formulate answers to the questions, begin your class discussion of the questions and the ideas presented by the questions. Be sure students take notes during the discussion so they have information to study for the unit test.

EXTRA WRITING ASSIGNMENTS/DISCUSSION QUESTIONS - *Black Boy*

Interpretation
1. From what point of view is *Black Boy* written, and what effect does that have on the story?

2. Is the story of *Black Boy* believable? Explain why or why not.

3. Where is the climax of the story? Explain your choice.

4. Are the characters in *Black Boy* stereotypes? If so, explain the usefulness of employing stereotypes in the novel. If they are not, explain how they merit individuality.

5. What is the setting of the story? Could this story have been set in a different time and place and still have the same effect?

Critical
6. Why do the members of Richard's family think he is a bad boy? Is he?

7. Are Richard's actions believably motivated? Explain why or why not.

8. Characterize Richard Wright's style of writing. How does it contribute to the value of the novel?

9. Describe Richard's relationship with his family.

10. Compare and contrast Richard and Shorty.

11. Explain how and why Richard is an individual different from other kids his age.

12. What forces shaped Richard into a writer? How?

13. In Chapter One and again in Chapter Two, Richard Wright created fairly long, almost poetic passages beginning with the words "There was." Find and reread these two passages. Explain the use and effect of these two sections.

14. Richard passes through several stages in the book. Define the stages he passes through as his character develops. Use examples from the text.

Black Boy Extra Discussion Questions page 2

15. It has been said that Wright wrote for two audiences in *Black Boy*: black and white. What was his message to each of these audiences, and was there any message intended for *both* audiences?

16. What faults in our society does Richard Wright point out in *Black Boy*?

17. Explain all the ways Richard was trapped, oppressed, in the South.

18. Many people say that Mr. Wright writes with a blues tone. Explain what that means. What are the "blues," and how does Mr. Wright's work reflect that style or tone?

Personal Response

19. Did you enjoy reading *Black Boy*? Why or why not?

20. Have you read *Native Son* by Richard Wright? If so, compare and contrast the two novels.

21. Do the things that happened to Richard still happen to Afro-Americans in the United States today? If so, why? If not, why not?

22. Are there places in the world where people are still oppressed and treated unjustly? Who, where, and how?

23. What was the most important idea you got from reading *Black Boy*?

24. Many books (both fact and fiction) have been written about the lives of Afro-Americans in America in the last century. Compare and contrast *Black Boy* with another such book you have read.

LESSON ELEVEN

Objective
> To review all of the vocabulary work done in this unit

Activity
> Choose one (or more) of the vocabulary review activities listed below and spend your class period as directed in the activity. Some of the materials for these review activities are located in the Extra Activities section of this unit.

VOCABULARY REVIEW ACTIVITIES

1. Divide your class into two teams and have an old-fashioned spelling or definition bee.

2. Give each of your students (or students in groups of two, three or four) a *Black Boy* Vocabulary Word Search Puzzle. The person (group) to find all of the vocabulary words in the puzzle first wins.

3. Give students a *Black Boy* Vocabulary Word Search Puzzle without the word list. The person or group to find the most vocabulary words in the puzzle wins.

4. Use a *Black Boy* Vocabulary Crossword Puzzle. Put the puzzle onto a transparency on the overhead projector (so everyone can see it), and do the puzzle together as a class.

5. Give students a *Black Boy* Vocabulary Matching Worksheet to do.

6. Divide your class into two teams. Use the *Black Boy* vocabulary words with their letters jumbled as a word list. Student 1 from Team A faces off against Student 1 from Team B. You write the first jumbled word on the board. The first student (1A or 1B) to unscramble the word wins the chance for his/her team to score points. If 1A wins the jumble, go to student 2A and give him/her a definition. He/she must give you the correct spelling of the vocabulary word which fits that definition. If he/she does, Team A scores a point, and you give student 3A a definition for which you expect a correctly spelled matching vocabulary word. Continue giving Team A definitions until some team member makes an incorrect response. An incorrect response sends the game back to the jumbled-word face off, this time with students 2A and 2B. Instead of repeating giving definitions to the first few students of each team, continue with the student after the one who gave the last incorrect response on the team. For example, if Team B wins the jumbled-word face-off, and student 5B gave the last incorrect answer for Team B, you would start this round of definition questions with student 6B, and so on. The team with the most points wins!

7. Have students write a story in which they correctly use as many vocabulary words as possible. Have students read their compositions orally. Post the most original compositions on your bulletin board.

LESSONS TWELVE AND THIRTEEN

Objectives
1. To study the ideas and themes in *Black Boy*
2. To give students the opportunity to work together in small groups
3. To help students review the text and find important ideas they may have missed on the first reading
4. To gather basic information which will be used in a discussion of the novel's themes

Activity #1
Divide your class into groups--one group for each of the following topics:

1. **Male Influences on Richard**: Nathaniel, Uncle Tom, Uncle Clark, Grandpa, Shorty, Olin, Reynolds and Pease, Crane, Falk, Griggs, Mencken, and Hoskins. Identify each of these characters and explain the influence each had on Richard.

2. **Female Influences on Richard**: Ella, Granny, Addie, Maggie, Miss Simon, Bess, Mrs. Moss, and Aunt Jody. Identify each of these characters and explain the influence each had on Richard.

3. **Freedom, Oppression, Slavery.** These are central to the themes and conflicts in the book. Explain how these three influences affected Richard's life. Give specific examples from the text.

4. **Food, Hunger, Strength**. Explore the roles of food, hunger, and strength in Richard's life.

5. **Religion.** Religion played a major role in Richard's life. Explain in what ways it affected him, how his views on religion were formed, and how the religious influences in his life helped form his whole viewpoint of life.

6. **Conflicts**. What are the conflicts in the book and how are they resolved (if they are resolved)?

7. **Education.** How is Richard educated? What are his views on education, his family's views, society's views? In what different ways is Richard educated?

Each group should look at its topic through the entire novel. Group members should divide the work into books, giving each person of the group a specific book to research. Each member should find all the references made to the group's topic within his/her section of the book. After each member has had time to complete his/her research, the group members should share their findings with each other. They should have a small group discussion to try to draw any reasonable conclusions they can from the data they collected. One group member should be designated "secretary" to jot down the group's ideas from the discussion. Another member should be designated "spokesperson" to report the group's ideas to the class.

Activity #2
The groups will each report their findings and conclusions to the whole class. The teacher or a student should write down on the board or overhead all of the findings and conclusions. Students should take notes for study use. Use the group reports as springboards for discussions of each of the topics assigned.

LESSONS FOURTEEN AND FIFTEEN

Objectives
1. To widen the breadth of students' knowledge about noteworthy authors
2. To check students' nonfiction reading assignments
3. To complete the project assignment

Activity
Ask each student to give a brief oral report about the information he/she read for the unit project assignment. Your criteria for evaluating this report will vary depending on the level of your students. You may wish for students to give a complete report without using notes of any kind, or you may want students to read directly from a written report, or you may want to do something in between these two extremes. Just make students aware of your criteria in ample time for them to prepare their reports.

LESSON SIXTEEN

Objectives
1. To give students the opportunity to practice writing to persuade
2. To help students review their nonfiction reading and prepare for the oral presentation
3. To give the teacher the opportunity to evaluate students' writing skills

Activity
Distribute Writing Assignment #3. Discuss the directions in detail and give students ample time to complete the assignment.

NOTES: Have many different persuasive articles -- any kind of persuasive writing -- available for students to read.

You may want to give students two class periods to work on this assignment, especially since they need to do a substantial amount of reading for it.

Be sure to tell students when their writing assignments will be due.

While students are working on Writing Assignment #3, call students to your desk or some other private area for individual writing conferences based on the first two writing assignments for this unit. An evaluation form is included for your convenience.

WRITING ASSIGNMENT #3 - *Black Boy*

PROMPT

"I opened *A Book of Prefaces* and began to read. I was jarred and shocked by the style, the clear, clean, sweeping sentences. Why did he write like that? And how did one write like that? I pictured the man as a raging demon, slashing with his pen, consumed with hate, denouncing everything American, extolling everything European or German, laughing at the weaknesses of people, mocking God, authority. What was this? I stood up, trying to realize what reality lay behind the meaning of the words. . . Yes, this man was fighting, fighting with words. He was using words as a weapon, using them as one would use a club. Could words be weapons? Well, yes, for here they were. Then, maybe, perhaps, I could use them as a weapon? No. It frightened me. I read on and what amazed me was not what he said, but how on earth anybody had the courage to say it."

Did you ever hear the old saying that the pen is mightier than the sword? In the passage above, Richard discovers the meaning of that old saying. Has it hit home to you yet, in your own life, that the more recent saying of, "He who has the most toys wins" is not the case. He who has the most words and can reach the most people with those words wins. Consider it.

Who are the most successful and influential people in our world? They are the ones who have convinced you (and millions of others) that they are right--whether they are political leaders, religious leaders, or leaders in business. How did the President get elected? He convinced the most people that he should be President. How do the Sunday Morning Preachers on television keep their media missions going? They convince people that their causes are the right ones and that they need money to keep their worthy causes going. People make donations and the Sunday Morning Preachers stay in business. What brand of jeans do you wear? Why? What kind of sneakers do you wear? Why? How did MacDonald's get to be #1? It convinced the most people that its food was the best and the fastest, and convinced millions--billions--of kids that Ronald MacDonald's place was the most fun, the best, the coolest place to be.

Here we are in the "information age"--a time in history when more information is readily accessible to more people than ever before. How will *you* use that information? If you have a computer, a modem, and a CD Rom drive, you have access to just about any information you can imagine--right at your fingertips. Successful people read. They figure out how to take the information they read and use it to further their own causes. Richard struck on this when he said, "Could words be weapons? . . . perhaps I could use them as a weapon?" YES! That is the point-- the point of an education, the point of learning to read, the point of learning to write. Take what you have learned and use it to help make your life and the lives of others better.

ASSIGNMENT

Write a composition in which you persuade me of something. Anything. Show me that you can use words for your own purposes.

NOTE: If there is something you have on your mind you would like to convince someone else about, feel free to use that topic and that audience.

Black Boy Writing Assignment #3 Page 2

PREWRITING

How will you persuade me? Begin by reading. How do other writers persuade their readers? Read at least five different persuasive articles--or any type of persuasive writing. Look at each article. For each article you read, fill out an Art of Persuasion Worksheet.

When your worksheets are done, study them. Then, using similar methods, create your own persuasive composition.

Of what do you want to convince me? What do you feel strongly enough about to try to get someone else to believe it? That's your topic.

How are you going to convince me? To what should you appeal? What argument(s) can you make that will "push the right buttons" to make me believe what you want me to believe? Jot down what arguments you think will be effective. Make a few notes next to each argument about comments, examples, explanations, etc., that would support your argument and appeal to me.

DRAFTING

Begin to write. An introductory paragraph is usually a good idea. You can either come right out with your point or you can be subtle, using other means to work your way around to your point. In your reading you probably saw examples of both styles. Do what you think will work best for your purposes.

In the body of your composition, you need to put forth your arguments.

Don't forget to write a concluding paragraph in which you use the essence of everything you've written to finally win me over to your viewpoint.

PROMPT

When you finish the rough draft of your paper, ask a student who sits near you to read it. After reading your rough draft, he/she should tell you what he/she liked best about your work, which parts were difficult to understand, and ways in which your work could be improved. Reread your paper considering your critic's comments and make the corrections you think are necessary.

PROOFREADING

Do a final proofreading of your paper double-checking your grammar, spelling, organization, and the clarity of your ideas.

THE ART OF PERSUASION WORKSHEET

Title of the article you read _____

Author of the article _____

Main point(s) of the article

_____

_____

_____

Arguments used in the article

_____

_____

_____

_____

Forms used in the article - Check all that apply.

    ( ) Examples?
    ( ) Stories?
    ( ) Negative arguments?
    ( ) Positive arguments?
    ( ) Comparison/contrast?
    ( ) Personal experience?
    ( ) Threats?
    ( ) Humor?
    ( ) Other (Explain _____

Did you think the author's points were valid?

Were you persuaded?

WRITING EVALUATION FORM - *Black Boy*

Name _____ Date _____

    Grade _____

Circle One For Each Item:

Grammar: correct   errors noted on paper

Spelling: correct   errors noted on paper

Punctuation: correct   errors noted on paper

Legibility: excellent   good   fair   poor

Strengths:

Weaknesses:

Comments/Suggestions:

LESSON SEVENTEEN

Objective
To review the main ideas presented in *Black Boy*

Activity #1
Choose one of the review games/activities included in this unit and spend your class period as outlined there. Some materials for these activities are located in the Extra Activities section of this unit.

Activity #2
Remind students that the Unit Test will be in the next class meeting. Stress the review of the Study Guides and their class notes as a last minute, brush-up review for homework.

REVIEW GAMES/ACTIVITIES - *Black Boy*

1. Ask the class to make up a unit test for *Black Boy*. The test should have 4 sections: matching, true/false, short answer, and essay. Students may use 1/2 period to make the test and then swap papers and use the other 1/2 class period to take a test a classmate has devised. (open book) You may want to use the unit test included in this packet or take questions from the students' unit tests to formulate your own test.

2. Take 1/2 period for students to make up true and false questions (including the answers). Collect the papers and divide the class into two teams. Draw a big tic-tac-toe board on the chalk board. Make one team X and one team O. Ask questions to each side, giving each student one turn. If the question is answered correctly, that students' team's letter (X or O) is placed in the box. If the answer is incorrect, no mark is placed in the box. The object is to get three marks in a row like tic-tac-toe. You may want to keep track of the number of games won for each team.

3. Take 1/2 period for students to make up questions (true/false and short answer). Collect the questions. Divide the class into two teams. You'll alternate asking questions to individual members of teams A & B (like in a spelling bee). The question keeps going from A to B until it is correctly answered, then a new question is asked. A correct answer does not allow the team to get another question. Correct answers are +2 points; incorrect answers are -1 point.

4. Have students pair up and quiz each other from their study guides and class notes.

5. Give students a *Black Boy* crossword puzzle to complete.

6. Divide your class into two teams. Use the *Black Boy* crossword words with their letters jumbled as a word list. Student 1 from Team A faces off against Student 1 from Team B. You write the first jumbled word on the board. The first student (1A or 1B) to unscramble the word wins the chance for his/her team to score points. If 1A wins the jumble, go to student 2A and give him/her a clue. He/she must give you the correct word which matches that clue. If he/she does, Team A scores a point, and you give student 3A a clue for which you expect another correct response. Continue giving Team A clues until some team member makes an incorrect response. An incorrect response sends the game back to the jumbled-word face off, this time with students 2A and 2B. Instead of repeating giving clues to the first few students of each team, continue with the student after the one who gave the last incorrect response on the team. For example, if Team B wins the jumbled-word face-off, and student 5B gave the last incorrect answer for Team B, you would start this round of clue questions with student 6B, and so on. The team with the most points wins!

LESSON EIGHTEEN

Objective
    To test the students understanding of the main ideas and themes in *Black Boy*

Activity #1
    Distribute the unit tests. Go over the instructions in detail and allow the students the entire class period to complete the exam.

NOTES ABOUT THE UNIT TESTS IN THIS UNIT:

    There are 5 different unit tests which follow.
    There are two short answer tests which are based primarily on facts from the novel.
    There is one advanced short answer unit test. It is based on the extra discussion questions and quotations. Use the matching key for short answer unit test 2 to check the matching section of the advanced short answer unit test. There is no key for the short answer questions and quotations. The answers will be based on the discussions you have had during class.
    There are two multiple choice unit tests. Following the two unit tests, you will find an answer sheet on which students should mark their answers. The same answer sheet should be used for both tests; however, students' answers will be different for each test. Following the students' answer sheet for the multiple choice tests you will find your answer keys.
    The short answer tests have a vocabulary section. You should choose 10 of the vocabulary words from this unit, read them orally and have the students write them down. Then, either have students write a definition or use the words in sentences.

    Use these words for the vocabulary section of the advanced short answer unit test:

aspirations	conspicuously	dubious	implacable
inconceivable	nonchalantly	petty	predilection
repugnant	surreptitiously	vivid	vindictive

Activity #2
    Collect all test papers and assigned books prior to the end of the class period.

UNIT TESTS

SHORT ANSWER UNIT TEST 1 - *Black Boy*

I. Matching

___ 1. Ella Wright   A. Richard's father

___ 2. Grandpa   B. Richard's classmate who gives him advice

___ 3. Aunt Addie   C. Head of the orphanage

___ 4. Harrison   D. Takes Richard to live with him in Greenwood

___ 5. Mrs. Moss   E. Richard's favorite aunt

___ 6. Reynolds   F. Strict Seventh-Day Adventist with whom Richard often lives

___ 7. Griggs   G. Richard's mother

___ 8. Miss Simon   H. Richard threatens him with razors

___ 9. Bess   I. Richard's landlady in Memphis

___ 10. Aunt Maggie   J. Elevator operator

___ 11. Granny   K. Author

___ 12. Uncle Clark   L. Granny's ally; Richard's teacher

___ 13. Uncle Thomas   M. Good-hearted white employer at optical company

___ 14. Mr. Crane   N. Sets up fight between Richard and Harrison

___ 15. Shorty   O. Threatens Richard and forces him to leave his good job

___ 16. Mr. Olin   P. Willing to marry Richard

___ 17. Mr. Falk   Q. Civil War veteran

___ 18. Nathaniel Wright   R. Helps Richard get library books

___ 19. Richard Wright   S. Agrees to fight Richard for money

Black Boy Short Answer Unit Test 1 Page 2

II. Short Answer

1. Why did Richard's mother let him go to the store even though she knew he might be beaten again?

2. Why didn't Granny want Richard to read story books?

3. What effect did Richard's mother's illness have on him?

4. Why did Richard write his first story?

5. Why did Richard sell the anti-Negro newspapers?

6. Who was Brother Manse, and what did Richard gain from his job with him?

7. Why didn't Richard want to work for the white woman who gave him moldy molasses?

Black Boy Short Answer Unit Test 1 Page 3

8. Why did Richard finally consent to being baptized into the church?

9. What did the North symbolize for Richard?

10. What effect did the death of Ned's brother, Bob, have on Richard?

11. Why did Richard refuse to deliver the pre-written graduation speech?

12. How did Richard get enough money to go North to Memphis?

Black Boy Short Answer Unit Test 1 Page 4

III. Essay

Explain how and why Richard was an "outsider" rejected by both blacks and whites.

Black Boy Short Answer Unit Test 1 Page 5

IV. Vocabulary

    Listen to the vocabulary words and write them down.
    Go back later and fill in the correct definition for each word.

1.

2.

3.

4.

5.

6.

7.

8.

9.

10.

SHORT ANSWER UNIT TEST 2 - *Black Boy*

I. Matching

___ 1. Ella Wright   A. Richard's landlady in Memphis

___ 2. Grandpa   B. Strict Seventh-Day Adventist with whom Richard often lives

___ 3. Aunt Addie   C. Author

___ 4. Harrison   D. Richard's classmate who gives him advice

___ 5. Mrs. Moss   E. Elevator operator

___ 6. Reynolds   F. Good-hearted white employer at optical company

___ 7. Griggs   G. Richard's father

___ 8. Miss Simon   H. Threatens Richard and forces him to leave his good job

___ 9. Bess   I. Willing to marry Richard

___ 10. Aunt Maggie   J. Civil War veteran

___ 11. Granny   K. Helps Richard get library books

___ 12. Uncle Clark   L. Takes Richard to live with him in Greenwood

___ 13. Uncle Thomas   M. Granny's ally; Richard's teacher

___ 14. Mr. Crane   N. Richard threatens him with razors

___ 15. Shorty   O. Richard's mother

___ 16. Mr. Olin   P. Head of the orphanage

___ 17. Mr. Falk   Q. Agrees to fight Richard for money

___ 18. Nathaniel Wright   R. Sets up fight between Richard and Harrison

___ 19. Richard Wright   S. Richard's favorite aunt

Black Boy Short Answer Unit Test 2 Page 2

II. Short Answer

1. On the trip to Arkansas, Richard becomes more aware of the separations between blacks and whites. When he asks his mother questions about racial differences, what is her reaction to him?

2. What effect did Richard's mother's illness have on him?

3. Why did Addie beat Richard, and what was his reaction?

4. Why didn't Richard want to work for the white woman who gave him moldy molasses?

5. What was The Voodoo of Hell's Half-Acre?

6. What did the North symbolize for Richard?

Black Boy Short Answer Unit Test 2 Page 3

7. Why did Richard refuse to deliver the pre-written graduation speech?

8. What three incidents left an impression on Richard during his time working at the clothing store?

9. What advice did Griggs give Richard?

10. Why did Richard resort to crime?

11. What author-editor intrigued Richard? Why?

12. How did Richard finally get to go North from Memphis?

Black Boy Short Answer Unit Test 2 Page 4

III. Composition
> Richard grew and learned from his experiences in the South.
> Explain what he learned and how he learned it.

Black Boy Short Answer Unit Test 2 Page 5

IV. Vocabulary

Listen to the vocabulary words and write them down. Go back later and fill in the correct definition for each word.

1.

2.

3.

4.

5.

6.

7.

8.

9.

10.

KEY: SHORT ANSWER UNIT TESTS - *Black Boy*

The short answer questions are taken directly from the study guides.
If you need to look up the answers, you will find them in the study guide section.

Answers to the composition questions will vary depending on your
class discussions and the level of your students.

For the vocabulary section of the test, choose ten of the
words from the vocabulary lists to read orally for your students.

The answers to the matching section of the test are below.

Answers to the matching section of the Advanced Short Answer Unit Test
are the same as for Short Answer Unit Test #2.

Test #1	Test #2
1. G	1. O
2. Q	2. J
3. L	3. M
4. S	4. Q
5. I	5. A
6. O	6. H
7. B	7. D
8. C	8. P
9. P	9. I
10. E	10. S
11. F	11. B
12. D	12. L
13. H	13. N
14. M	14. F
15. J	15. E
16. N	16. R
17. R	17. K
18. A	18. G
19. K	19. C

ADVANCED SHORT ANSWER UNIT TEST - *Black Boy*

I. Matching

___ 1. Ella Wright   A. Richard's landlady in Memphis

___ 2. Grandpa   B. Strict Seventh-Day Adventist with whom Richard often lives

___ 3. Aunt Addie   C. Author

___ 4. Harrison   D. Richard's classmate who gives him advice

___ 5. Mrs. Moss   E. Elevator operator

___ 6. Reynolds   F. Good-hearted white employer at optical company

___ 7. Griggs   G. Richard's father

___ 8. Miss Simon   H. Threatens Richard and forces him to leave his good job

___ 9. Bess   I. Willing to marry Richard

___ 10. Aunt Maggie   J. Civil War veteran

___ 11. Granny   K. Helps Richard get library books

___ 12. Uncle Clark   L. Takes Richard to live with him in Greenwood

___ 13. Uncle Thomas   M. Granny's ally; Richard's teacher

___ 14. Mr. Crane   N. Richard threatens him with razors

___ 15. Shorty   O. Richard's mother

___ 16. Mr. Olin   P. Head of the orphanage

___ 17. Mr. Falk   Q. Agrees to fight Richard for money

___ 18. Nathaniel Wright   R. Sets up fight between Richard and Harrison

___ 19. Richard Wright   S. Richard's favorite aunt

Black Boy Advanced Short Answer Unit Test Page 2

II. Short Answer

1. Why do the members of Richard's family think he is a bad boy? Is he?

2. Describe Richard's relationship with his family.

3. Compare and contrast Richard and Shorty.

4. Explain how and why Richard is an individual different from other kids his age.

5. What forces shaped Richard into a writer? How?

Black Boy Advanced Short Answer Unit Test Page 3

6. Richard passes through several stages in the book. Define the stages he passes through as his character develops. Use examples from the text.

7. Explain all the ways Richard was trapped, oppressed, in the South.

8. How did H. L. Mencken influence Richard?

9. Describe the role of religion in Richard's life.

10. Describe how Richard got his education -- both the school type of education and education about life.

Black Boy Advanced Short Answer Unit Test Page 4

III. Composition

    What was Richard's main problem? Did he eventually solve it? If so, how? If not, why not? Defend your answer thoroughly using examples from the text to support your statements.

Black Boy Advanced Short Answer Unit Test Page 5

IV. Vocabulary

    Write down the vocabulary words you are given. Go back later and use all of those vocabulary words in a short composition relating to *Black Boy*.

MULTIPLE CHOICE UNIT TEST 1 - *Black Boy*

I. Matching

___ 1. Ella Wright   A. Richard's father

___ 2. Grandpa   B. Richard's classmate who gives him advice

___ 3. Aunt Addie   C. Head of the orphanage

___ 4. Harrison   D. Takes Richard to live with him in Greenwood

___ 5. Mrs. Moss   E. Richard's favorite aunt

___ 6. Reynolds   F. Strict Seventh-Day Adventist with whom Richard often lives

___ 7. Griggs   G. Richard's mother

___ 8. Miss Simon   H. Richard threatens him with razors

___ 9. Bess   I. Richard's landlady in Memphis

___ 10. Aunt Maggie   J. Elevator operator

___ 11. Granny   K. Author

___ 12. Uncle Clark   L. Granny's ally; Richard's teacher

___ 13. Uncle Thomas   M. Good-hearted white employer at optical company

___ 14. Mr. Crane   N. Sets up fight between Richard and Harrison

___ 15. Shorty   O. Threatens Richard and forces him to leave his good job

___ 16. Mr. Olin   P. Willing to marry Richard

___ 17. Mr. Falk   Q. Civil War veteran

___ 18. Nathaniel Wright   R. Helps Richard get library books

___ 19. Richard Wright   S. Agrees to fight Richard for money

Black Boy Multiple Choice Unit Test 1 Page 2

II. Multiple Choice

1. Why did Richard's mother make him go to the store even though she knew he might be beaten again?
    A. She was desperate for food but was afraid to go to the store herself.
    B. She subconsciously hoped he would be killed, so that she would not have to take care of him any more.
    C. She was teaching him to stand up for himself, to survive in the real world.
    D. She was drunk and didn't realize what she was doing.

2. What did Richard do to pass the time of day when he was six years old?
    A. He went to the local saloon where people bought him drinks and urged him to repeat obscenities.
    B. He beat up the younger children in the neighborhood and stole their food.
    C. He hid out in the library and taught himself to read.
    D. He visited the elderly neighbors and begged for food.

3. What happened to Richard when his mother became ill?
    A. He went to reform school.
    B. He went to live with his father.
    C. He lived by himself on the streets.
    D. He went to live in an orphanage.

4. On the trip to Arkansas, Richard becomes more aware of the separations between blacks and whites. When he asks his mother questions about racial differences, what is her reaction to him?
    A. She quietly and calmly tells him everything she knows.
    B. She ignores him and refuses to answer at all.
    C. She brushes his questions off with a few bare facts.
    D. She tells him there are no differences, that the idea is all in his imagination.

5. What forced Richard to ask to leave Greenwood?
    A. He was afraid of his aunt because she was constantly threatening to beat him. She was also starting to force him to steal things at the local grocery store. He knew he had to get away from her.
    B. He couldn't learn in school. The principal refused to promote him to the next grade, and he was too embarrassed to stay in a class where he was the oldest.
    C. He got in trouble with the neighborhood gang and was afraid he would be killed.
    D. He found out that a boy had died in the bed in which he slept. He didn't want to sleep in the bed and wasn't permitted to sleep anywhere else. He became exhausted and asked to be returned to his mother.

Black Boy Multiple Choice Unit Test 1 Page 3

6. Why did Richard write his first story?
   A. He was bored with prayer and writing gave him an escape from his oppressive life.
   B. There was a contest at school, and he wanted to win the $10 prize.
   C. He was trying to impress a girl in his class who was very studious.
   D. He did it to defy Granny.

7. Why did Richard sell the anti-Negro newspapers?
   A. His grandmother forced him to do it?
   B. It was his misguided form of social protest.
   C. He didn't know the content; he just wanted to read the magazine section of stories and to make a little money.
   D. Some white boys he knew had threatened to hurt his mother and grandmother if he didn't sell the papers.

8. What did Richard gain from his association with Brother Manse?
   A. He learned the insurance business.
   B. He made a lot of money that enabled him to move out of his grandmother's house.
   C. He gained thirty pounds because Brother Manse was always feeding him.
   D. He gained a new outlook on life and a little self-respect.

9. Why did Richard finally consent to being baptized into the church?
   A. He did it out of love for his mother, so she wouldn't be humiliated.
   B. His friends were putting pressure on him to join.
   C. He honestly believed he had "gotten the faith."
   D. He was too run down and tired to argue any more.

10. Richard said one particular place symbolized "...all that I had not felt and seen; it had no relation whatever to what actually existed. Yet, by imagining a place where everything was possible, I kept hope alive in me."   What was this place?
    A. It was the white area of the city.
    B. It was heaven.
    C. It was the North.
    D. It was the world he was creating in his writing.

11. Why did Richard refuse to deliver the pre-written graduation speech?
    A. He felt that his speech should be his own instead of a piece prepared by others for social or political reasons.
    B. He was ashamed to admit he couldn't read it.
    C. He didn't want to be set apart from the other boys.
    D. It was his form of protest, to let the school officials know that he thought he had received an inadequate education.

Black Boy Multiple Choice Unit Test 1 Page 4

12. Why did Richard resort to crime?
    A. He really wanted to get arrested. He had heard that in jail he would have a warm place to live, clean clothes, and regular meals. This was appealing to him.
    B. He found out he liked the thrill of it. It was the only part of his existence where he really felt alive.
    C. He was under pressure from his family and friends to do so.
    D. He could not honestly earn enough to live and save money. He felt as though he had no choice.

13. How did Richard manage to get books from the library?
    A. He made arrangements with a Catholic white man at work, Mr. Falk, to pretend to be sent from Falk to get books from the library.
    B. He became friends with the cleaning woman. She sneaked the books out to him at night.
    C. He offered to work the library for free in return for the privilege of borrowing books.
    D. He started following the librarian home at night. He threatened to hurt her if she didn't bring him books. She complied.

14. What effect did the library books have on Richard?
    A. They made him even angrier and more frustrated with his situation.
    B. They numbed him and kept him from thinking about reality.
    C. They gave him hope and educated him.
    D. They made him feel superior to the other blacks he knew, and then he felt very isolated. He stopped reading.

15. How did Richard finally get enough money to go North?
    a. He resorted to crime, and took money from the ticket sales at the theater.
    b. Mr. Falk paid his way.
    c. His mother died and he used the insurance money.
    d. He never had enough money; he jumped on a freight train headed for Illinois.

Black Boy Multiple Choice Unit Test 1 Page 5

III. Composition
    What did Richard Wright accomplish by writing *Black Boy*?

Black Boy Multiple Choice Unit Test 1 Page 6

IV. Vocabulary - Match the correct definitions to the words.

____ 1. ASPIRATIONS   A. Hostility that results in active resistance or oppression

____ 2. FEIGNED   B. Had a strong, often melancholy desire

____ 3. MOROSE   C. Impossible to please or satisfy

____ 4. YEARNED   D. Gloomy

____ 5. WANED   E. Gave a false appearance of; pretended

____ 6. FRENZY   F. A state of violent or wild excitement

____ 7. IMPLORING   G. Something that incites or is intended to cause trouble

____ 8. INDULGENTLY   H. Ambitions

____ 9. ANXIETY   I. Suppositional

____ 10. WAYLAYING   J. Scornful

____ 11. SAUCILY   K. Causing to appear guilty of a crime or fault

____ 12. TANTAMOUNT   L. Ambushing; intercepting someone unexpectedly

____ 13. PROVOCATIONS   M. Approached an end

____ 14. CRYPTIC   N. Leniently; patiently

____ 15. INCRIMINATING   O. Equivalent in effect or value

____ 16. CONTEMPTUOUS   P. Disrespectfully

____ 17. IMPLACABLE   Q. A state of uneasiness and apprehension

____ 18. HYPOTHETICAL   R. Tending to conceal or camouflage

____ 19. ANTAGONISM   S. Making an earnest appeal

____ 20. QUALMS   T. Uneasy feelings about the rightness of an action

MULTIPLE CHOICE UNIT TEST 2 - *Black Boy*

___ 1. Ella Wright   A. Richard's landlady in Memphis

___ 2. Grandpa   B. Strict Seventh-Day Adventist with whom Richard often lives

___ 3. Aunt Addie   C. Author

___ 4. Harrison   D. Richard's classmate who gives him advice

___ 5. Mrs. Moss   E. Elevator operator

___ 6. Reynolds   F. Good-hearted white employer at optical company

___ 7. Griggs   G. Richard's father

___ 8. Miss Simon   H. Threatens Richard and forces him to leave his good job

___ 9. Bess   I. Willing to marry Richard

___ 10. Aunt Maggie   J. Civil War veteran

___ 11. Granny   K. Helps Richard get library books

___ 12. Uncle Clark   L. Takes Richard to live with him in Greenwood

___ 13. Uncle Thomas   M. Granny's ally; Richard's teacher

___ 14. Mr. Crane   N. Richard threatens him with razors

___ 15. Shorty   O. Richard's mother

___ 16. Mr. Olin   P. Head of the orphanage

___ 17. Mr. Falk   Q. Agrees to fight Richard for money

___ 18. Nathaniel Wright   R. Sets up fight between Richard and Harrison

___ 19. Richard Wright   S. Richard's favorite aunt

Black Boy Multiple Choice Unit Test 2 Page 2

II. Multiple Choice

1. Why did Richard's mother make him go to the store even though she knew he might be beaten again?
    - A. She was desperate for food but was afraid to go to the store herself.
    - B. She subconsciously hoped he would be killed, so that she would not have to take care of him any more.
    - C. She was drunk and didn't realize what she was doing.
    - D. She was teaching him to stand up for himself, to survive in the real world.

2. What did Richard do to pass the time of day when he was six years old?
    - A. He beat up the younger children in the neighborhood and stole their food.
    - B. He went to the local saloon where people bought him drinks and urged him to repeat obscenities.
    - C. He hid out in the library and taught himself to read.
    - D. He visited the elderly neighbors and begged for food.

3. What happened to Richard when his mother became ill?
    - A. He went to reform school.
    - B. He went to live with his father.
    - C. He went to live in an orphanage.
    - D. He lived by himself on the streets.

4. On the trip to Arkansas, Richard becomes more aware of the separations between blacks and whites. When he asks his mother questions about racial differences, what is her reaction to him?
    - A. She quietly and calmly tells him everything she knows.
    - B. She brushes his questions off with a few bare facts.
    - C. She ignores him and refuses to answer at all.
    - D. She tells him there are no differences, that the idea is all in his imagination.

5. What forced Richard to ask to leave Greenwood?
    - A. He found out that a boy had died in the bed in which he slept. He didn't want to sleep in the bed and wasn't permitted to sleep anywhere else. He became exhausted and asked to be returned to his mother.
    - B. He couldn't learn in school. The principal refused to promote him to the next grade, and he was too embarrassed to stay in a class where he was the oldest.
    - C. He got in trouble with the neighborhood gang and was afraid he would be killed.
    - D. He was afraid of his aunt because she was constantly threatening to beat him. She was also starting to force him to steal things at the local grocery store. He knew he had to get away from her.

Black Boy Multiple Choice Unit Test 2 Page 3

6. Why did Richard write his first story?
    A. There was a contest at school and he wanted to win the $10 prize.
    B. He was bored with prayer, and writing gave him an escape from his oppressive life.
    C. He was trying to impress a girl in his class who was very studious.
    D. He did it to defy Granny.

7. Why did Richard sell the anti-Negro newspapers?
    A. He didn't know the content; he just wanted to read the magazine section of stories and to make a little money.
    B. It was his misguided form of social protest.
    C. His grandmother forced him to do it.
    D. Some white boys he knew had threatened to hurt his mother and grandmother if he didn't sell the papers.

8. What did Richard gain from his association with Brother Manse?
    A. He learned the insurance business.
    B. He made a lot of money that enabled him to move out of his grandmother's house.
    C. He gained a new outlook on life and a little self-respect.
    D. He gained thirty pounds because Brother Manse was always feeding him.

9. Why did Richard finally consent to being baptized into the church?
    A. His friends were putting pressure on him to join.
    B. He did it out of love for his mother, so she wouldn't be humiliated.
    C. He honestly believed he had "gotten the faith."
    D. He was too run down and tired to argue any more.

10. Richard said one particular place symbolized "...all that I had not felt and seen; it had no relation whatever to what actually existed. Yet, by imagining a place where everything was possible, I kept hope alive in me."   What was this place?
    A. It was the white area of the city.
    B. It was heaven.
    C. It was the world he was creating in his writing.
    D. It was the North.

11. Why did Richard refuse to deliver the pre-written graduation speech?
    A. It was his form of protest, to let the school officials know that he thought he had received an inadequate education.
    B. He was ashamed to admit he couldn't read it.
    C. He didn't want to be set apart from the other boys.
    D. He felt that his speech should be his own instead of a piece prepared by others for social or political reasons.

Black Boy Multiple Choice Unit Test 2 Page 4

12. Why did Richard resort to crime?
    A. He could not honestly earn enough to live and save money. He felt as though he had no choice.
    B. He found out he liked the thrill of it. It was the only part of his existence where he really felt alive.
    C. He was under pressure from his family and friends to do so.
    D. He really wanted to get arrested. He had heard that in jail he would have a warm place to live, clean clothes, and regular meals. This was appealing to him.

13. How did Richard manage to get books from the library?
    A. He became friends with the cleaning woman. She sneaked the books out to him at night.
    B. He made arrangements with a Catholic white man at work, Mr. Falk, to pretend to be sent from Falk to get books from the library.
    C. He offered to work the library for free in return for the privilege of borrowing books.
    D. He started following the librarian home at night. He threatened to hurt her if she didn't bring him books. She complied.

14. What effect did the library books have on Richard?
    A. They made him even angrier and more frustrated with his situation.
    B. They gave him hope and educated him.
    C. They numbed him and kept him from thinking about reality.
    D. They made him feel superior to the other blacks he knew, and then he felt very isolated. He stopped reading.

15. How did Richard finally get enough money to go North?
    a. His mother died and he used the insurance money.
    b. Mr. Falk paid his way.
    c. He resorted to crime, and took money from the ticket sales at the theater.
    d. He never had enough money; he jumped on a freight train headed for Illinois.

Black Boy Multiple Choice Unit Test 2 Page 5

III. Composition

"I knew that I could never really leave the South, for my feelings had already been formed by the South, for there had been slowly instilled into my personality and consciousness, black though I was, the culture of the South."

Explain Richard Wright's statement using examples from the text.

Black Boy Multiple Choice Unit Test 2 Page 6

IV. Vocabulary - Match the correct definitions to the words.

_____ 1. MOROSE   A. An impelling force

_____ 2. CONSPICUOUSLY   B. Obviously

_____ 3. TAUT   C. Excited as to anger or action; stirred up

_____ 4. NUANCE   D. Being subordinate; of a lesser position

_____ 5. BOON   E. Looking intently or searchingly

_____ 6. ROUSED   F. Going to as a customer

_____ 7. ENTHRALLED   G. A secret or underhanded scheme

_____ 8. INTRIGUE   H. Lowered in character, quality or value

_____ 9. PEERING   I. Ambitions

_____ 10. SUBSERVIENCE   J. Equivalent in effect or value

_____ 11. CONTEMPTUOUS   K. Tight; tense

_____ 12. TANTAMOUNT   L. Abusive language

_____ 13. IMPETUS   M. Uneasy feelings about the rightness of an action

_____ 14. INVECTIVES   N. Gave a false appearance of; pretended

_____ 15. PATRONIZING   O. A benefit

_____ 16. FEIGNED   P. Scornful

_____ 17. QUALMS   Q. Subtle or slight degree of difference

_____ 18. DEBASED   R. Gloomy

_____ 19. DEVOID   S. Spellbound; captivated

_____ 20. ASPIRATIONS   T. Completely lacking or empty

ANSWER SHEET - *Black Boy*
Multiple Choice Unit Tests

I. Matching	II. Multiple Choice	IV. Vocabulary
1. ___	1. ___	1. ___
2. ___	2. ___	2. ___
3. ___	3. ___	3. ___
4. ___	4. ___	4. ___
5. ___	5. ___	5. ___
6. ___	6. ___	6. ___
7. ___	7. ___	7. ___
8. ___	8. ___	8. ___
9. ___	9. ___	9. ___
10. ___	10. ___	10. ___
11. ___	11. ___	11. ___
12. ___	12. ___	12. ___
13. ___	13. ___	13. ___
14. ___	14. ___	14. ___
15. ___	15. ___	15. ___
16. ___		16. ___
17. ___		17. ___
18. ___		18. ___
19. ___		19. ___
		20. ___

ANSWER KEY - *Black Boy*
Multiple Choice Unit Tests

Answers to Unit Test 1 are in the left column. Answers to Unit Test 2 are in the right column.

I. Matching	II. Multiple Choice	IV. Vocabulary
1. G O	1. C D	1. H R
2. Q J	2. A B	2. E B
3. L M	3. D C	3. D K
4. S Q	4. C B	4. B Q
5. I A	5. D A	5. M O
6. O H	6. A B	6. F C
7. B D	7. C A	7. S S
8. C P	8. A A	8. N G
9. P I	9. A B	9. O E
10. E S	10. C D	10. L D
11. F B	11. A D	11. P P
12. D L	12. D A	12. O J
13. H N	13. A B	13. G A
14. M F	14. C B	14. R L
15. J E	15. A C	15. K F
16. N R		16. J N
17. R K		17. C M
18. A G		18. I H
19. K C		19. A T
		20. T I

UNIT RESOURCE MATERIALS

BULLETIN BOARD IDEAS - *Black Boy*

1. Save one corner of the board for the best of students' *Black Boy* writing assignments.

2. Take one of the word search puzzles from the extra activities section and, with a marker, copy it over in a large size on the bulletin board. Write the clue words to find to one side. Invite students prior to and after class to find the words and circle them on the bulletin board.

3. Write several of the most significant quotations from the book onto the board on brightly colored paper.

4. Make a bulletin board listing the vocabulary words for this unit. As you complete sections of the novel and discuss the vocabulary for each section, write the definitions on the bulletin board. (If your board is one students face frequently, it will help them learn the words.)

5. Do a bulletin board about ways to deal with stress, anger and frustration.

6. Use the bulletin board suggested in the introductory lesson.

7. Make a bulletin board about the history of the Civil Rights Movement.

8. Make a bulletin board on which you post pictures and short biographies of famous black authors, including Richard Wright.

EXTRA ACTIVITIES - *Black Boy*

One of the difficulties in teaching a novel is that all students don't read at the same speed. One student who likes to read may take the book home and finish it in a day or two. Sometimes a few students finish the in-class assignments early. The problem, then, is finding suitable extra activities for students.

The best thing I've found is to keep a little library in the classroom. For this unit on *Black Boy,* you might check out from the school library other related books and articles about the civil rights movement, H. L. Mencken, the naturalists and their works, Marxism, or information about coping with stress and anger. Other books by Richard Wright would be helpful. Also consider articles of criticism about *Black Boy*.

Other things you may keep on hand are puzzles. We have made some relating directly to *Black Boy* for you. Feel free to duplicate them.

Some students may like to draw. You might devise a contest or allow some extra-credit grade for students who draw characters or scenes from *Black Boy*. Note, too, that if the students do not want to keep their drawings you may pick up some extra bulletin board materials this way. If you have a contest and you supply the prize (a CD or something like that perhaps), you could, possibly, make the drawing itself a non-returnable entry fee.

The pages which follow contain games, puzzles and worksheets. The keys, when appropriate, immediately follow the puzzle or worksheet. There are two main groups of activities: one group for the unit; that is, generally relating to the *Black Boy* text, and another group of activities related strictly to the *Black Boy* vocabulary.

Directions for these games, puzzles and worksheets are self-explanatory. The object here is to provide you with extra materials you may use in any way you choose.

MORE ACTIVITIES - Black Boy

1. Pick a chapter or scene with a great deal of dialogue and have the students act it out on a stage. (Perhaps you could assign various scenes to different groups of students so more than one scene could be acted and more students could participate.)

2. Have students design a book cover (front and back and inside flaps) for *Black Boy*.

3. Have students design a bulletin board (ready to be put up; not just sketched) for *Black Boy*.

4. Use some of the related topics noted earlier for an in-class library as topics for research, reports or written papers, or as topics for guest speakers.

5. Do a little survey in your class. Find out how many of your students have jobs. Use that as a springboard for discussion about attitudes towards jobs and the role of work in the life of a teenager. (Is it important to have a job? What does one gain from having a job? Why do those who work do so? Why do some students work and others not?)

6. Have students research and discuss careers in journalism, or careers that center around writing in general -- advertising, technical writing, etc.

7. Have students read another work of fiction that deals with the same theme(s) as *Black Boy* and have students compare the work they read to *Black Boy*.

8. Have students generate a list of the problems facing black Americans today. Have students meet in small groups to brainstorm effective ways of overcoming the problems.

9. Like Richard Wright, many authors in the period from 1920-1940 went to Europe to live -- or frequently visited there. Have students research who went there and why they went.

WORD SEARCH - *Black Boy*

All words in this list are associated with *Black Boy*. The words are placed backwards, forward, diagonally, up and down. The included words are listed below the word searches.

```
N C O U N T A S D K G X H R J J Q K N N R V S W
C O P K M Q L N R E Z R L F B M R D S O C S N N
G V O C C S L J G B A T A B W Y E A E Y M I B M
Q G S L M E N C K E N T S N Y I P H Z L L I X S
C U R T A I N S F A L K H M D R E Y N O L D S F
G R G T S S B I N O V E Z G E P L D T L R A Y N
B T A R F X N E B L E M V T I L A T E R M S A W
R A B N I K I M N G D S E A A R K S D O O T Z S
R D P C E G Y R D Y E N O M T G W L H T H H M T
C L P T G S G U W T D S D L T O X T U A H P S C
X V Q A I K J S O R S H J O D H R N N F C P Z G
T B M J S Z G W D R T H S N O I I I Q L N K Q N
B S I H P M E M S R E P A P S W E N A D D I E L
P E O H E L H D O H A H P R V L N R K W Z T S G
Z T S H C L K N Y W P H P S R O K E S H T Q J Y
J J B S Q E E Q M R N Q C F T I O Y E I B J S C
G R A N N Y E N O A S B K I X T S D K R M O S S
J B W U C J B P A H R P P Y R S M O O C G B T R
J X E C N A R U S N I R D B C R C F N O Q Y Z F
M B Z D R T R Y W Z R B Y F G B J W V D G F J L
```

ADDIE	FALK	MENCKEN	SHORTY
ALLY	GRANDPA	MONEY	SHOT
ANGEL	GRANNY	MOSS	SIMON
AUNT	GREENWOOD	NATHANIEL	SINFUL
BAPTIZED	GRIGGS	NEWSPAPERS	SOLDIERS
BESS	HARRISON	NORTH	SPEECH
CLARK	HELENA	OLIN	SYMBOL
COUNT	INSURANCE	ORPHAN	THINK
CRANE	JUDGE	PRETEND	THOMAS
CURTAINS	KITTEN	RAZORS	TOWEL
DEATH	KNIFE	REYNOLDS	VOODOO
DIED	MAGGIE	RICHARD	WRIGHT
ELEVATOR	MARRY	SALOON	
ELLA	MEMPHIS	SELL	

CROSSWORD - *Black Boy*

CROSSWORD CLUES - *Black Boy*

ACROSS

1. Strict Seventh-Day Adventist with whom Richard often lives
5. Addie or Maggie to Richard
7. Richard was the author's first ----
10. Agrees to fight Richard for money
11. Brother Manse's work
13. Richard hanged it to get back at his father
14. Short head movement meaning 'yes'
15. Given freedom
16. Takes Richard to live in Greenwood
17. White men --- Uncle Hoskins
19. Ire; rage
20. Nickname for mother
21. 'The penalty of --- awaited me if I made a false move ....'
23. Richard took part in a scheme that skimmed -- from ticket sales
25. Granny hit Richard with one when he told her to 'kiss back there'
28. Willing to marry Richard
30. Uncle Clark & Aunt Jody lived there
32. Richard's mother
34. Friend
35. Richard threatened him with razors
37. Belonging to it
38. Richard had to live -- from his mother; away
39. Allow
40. Revise, as in writing
43. Richard had to go to an ---'s home when his mother became ill
44. Richard and Harrison agreed to --- to fight
48. Granny's ally; Richard's teacher
50. Richard threatened to cut Uncle Tom with ---
52. Richard sold 'anti-Negro' -----
54. Mrs. Moss wanted Bess to --- Richard
55. With ingenuity
56. Belonging to me
57. Possess

DOWN

1. Richard's classmate who gives him advice
2. 'It symbolized to me all I had not felt and seen ....'
3. Civil War veteran
4. A boy had -- in Richard's bed at Uncle Clark's house
5. If Richard had seen an --- like Jacob had, he would have believed, too
6. Advice Griggs gave Richard
7. Richard's father
8. Author/editor who intrigued Richard
9. Richard defended himself against Aunt Addie with one
10. Wrights had to move from West ---
12. Place where Richard passed time at age 6
16. Good-hearted white employer at optical company
18. Unusual
22. The coal man taught Richard to ---
23. Richard's favorite aunt
24. Shorty operated one
26. Landlady in Memphis
27. Home town of Mrs. Moss and Bess
28. Richard agreed to be --- into the church to please his mother
29. Richard tried to --- Bessie
31. Author's last name
33. Helped Richard get library books
36. Set up fight between Richard and Harrison
41. Ruled in Richard's father's favor in court
42. Elevator operator
44. Richard --- through the wall into the next room
45. Opposite of more difficult
46. Make able to
47. 'The ---- of Hell's Half-Acre'
48. Aunt Addie was Granny's ---
49. Make a mistake
51. Head of the orphanage
53. Pretend to be something you aren't

CROSSWORD ANSWER KEY - *Black Boy*

MATCHING QUIZ/WORKSHEET 1 - *Black Boy*

____ 1. ALLY   A. Richard's mother

____ 2. SALOON   B. Richard refused to deliver the prewritten graduation -----

____ 3. SOLDIERS   C. Home town of Mrs. Moss and Bess

____ 4. GREENWOOD   D. Richard saw these & prisoners when returning to Granny's

____ 5. INSURANCE   E. White men --- Uncle Hoskins

____ 6. ADDIE   F. Threatened Richard & forced him to leave his good job

____ 7. BESS   G. Richard's father

____ 8. SHOT   H. Richard had to go to an ---'s home when his mother became ill

____ 9. PRETEND   I. Place where Richard passed time at age 6

____ 10. GRANNY   J. Uncle Clark & Aunt Jody lived there

____ 11. ELEVATOR   K. Strict Seventh-Day Adventist with whom Richard often lives

____ 12. ORPHAN   L. Landlady in Memphis

____ 13. NATHANIEL   M. Author's last name

____ 14. HARRISON   N. Willing to marry Richard

____ 15. SPEECH   O. Brother Manse's work

____ 16. MEMPHIS   P. Agrees to fight Richard for money

____ 17. ELLA   Q. Shorty operated one

____ 18. MOSS   R. Richard and Harrison agreed to --- to fight

____ 19. WRIGHT   S. Granny's ally; Richard's teacher

____ 20. REYNOLDS   T. Aunt Addie was Granny's —

MATCHING QUIZ/WORKSHEET 2 - *Black Boy*

____ 1. PRETEND   A. Addie or Maggie to Richard

____ 2. MARRY   B. Place where Richard passed time at age 6

____ 3. RICHARD   C. Richard's classmate who gives him advice

____ 4. AUNT   D. Landlady in Memphis

____ 5. GRIGGS   E. The coal man taught Richard to ---

____ 6. GRANDPA   F. Richard tried to --- Bessie

____ 7. COUNT   G. Richard's mother

____ 8. SELL   H. 'My mother's suffering grew into a --- in my mind ....'

____ 9. SPEECH   I. Wrights had to move from West ---

____ 10. ELEVATOR   J. Richard refused to deliver the prewritten graduation -----

____ 11. WRIGHT   K. Takes Richard to live in Greenwood

____ 12. REYNOLDS   L. Set up fight between Richard and Harrison

____ 13. HELENA   M. Mrs. Moss wanted Bess to --- Richard

____ 14. SALOON   N. Civil War veteran

____ 15. MOSS   O. Shorty operated one

____ 16. OLIN   P. Threatened Richard & forced him to leave his good job

____ 17. TOWEL   Q. Richard and Harrison agreed to --- to fight

____ 18. SYMBOL   R. Author's last name

____ 19. CLARK   S. Granny hit Richard with one when he told her to 'kiss back there'

____ 20. ELLA   T. *Black Boy* is about him

KEY: MATCHING QUIZ/WORKSHEETS - *Black Boy*

Worksheet 1	Worksheet 2
1. T	1. Q
2. I	2. M
3. D	3. T
4. J	4. A
5. O	5. C
6. S	6. N
7. N	7. E
8. E	8. F
9. R	9. J
10. K	10. O
11. Q	11. R
12. H	12. P
13. G	13. I
14. P	14. B
15. B	15. D
16. C	16. L
17. A	17. S
18. L	18. H
19. M	19. K
20. F	20. G

JUGGLE LETTER REVIEW GAME CLUE SHEET - *Black Boy*

SCRAMBLED	WORD	CLUE
IDEAD	ADDIE	Granny's ally; Richard's teacher
LALY	ALLY	Aunt Addie was Granny's ---
LAGEN	ANGEL	If Richard had seen an --- like Jacob had, he would have believed, too
TUNA	AUNT	Addie or Maggie to Richard
ZIPDEBAT	BAPTIZED	Richard agreed to be --- into the church to please his mother
SEBS	BESS	Willing to marry Richard
RKALC	CLARK	Takes Richard to live in Greenwood
TONCU	COUNT	The coal man taught Richard to ---
EARNC	CRANE	Good-hearted white employer at optical company
SIRTACNU	CURTAINS	Little Richard set these on fire
HEADT	DEATH	'The penalty of --- awaited me if I made a false move ....'
EDDI	DIED	A boy had -- in Richard's bed at Uncle Clark's house
RALEEVOT	ELEVATOR	Shorty operated one
LALE	ELLA	Richard's mother
LKFA	FALK	Helped Richard get library books
DANGPAR	GRANDPA	Civil War veteran
RAGYNN	GRANNY	Strict Seventh-Day Adventist with whom Richard often lives
NEWORGODE	GREENWOOD	Uncle Clark & Aunt Jody lived there
SIRGGG	GRIGGS	Richard's classmate who gives him advice
NISHAROR	HARRISON	Agrees to fight Richard for money
HEELAN	HELENA	Wrights had to move from West ---
CIRNUENAS	INSURANCE	Brother Manse's work
DEJGU	JUDGE	Ruled in Richard's father's favor in court
ITKENT	KITTEN	Richard hanged it to get back at his father
FINEK	KNIFE	Richard defended himself against Aunt Addie with one
GAMEIG	MAGGIE	Richard's favorite aunt
ARRYM	MARRY	Mrs. Moss wanted Bess to --- Richard
SHIMPME	MEMPHIS	Home town of Mrs. Moss and Bess
NMKEECN	MENCKEN	Author/editor who intrigued Richard
ONEYM	MONEY	Richard took part in a scheme that skimmed -- from ticket sales
SMSO	MOSS	Landlady in Memphis
ITENANHLA	NATHANIEL	Richard's father

Black Boy Juggle Letter Review Game Continued

ESPRWEPNAS	NEWSPAPERS	Richard sold 'anti-Negro' -----
TROHN	NORTH	'It symbolized to me all I had not felt and seen ....'
NOIL	OLIN	Set up fight between Richard and Harrison
NOPARH	ORPHAN	Richard had to go to an ---'s home when his mother became ill
EDPTRNE	PRETEND	Richard and Harrison agreed to --- to fight
ZORRAS	RAZORS	Richard threatened to cut Uncle Tom with —
YSDOERNL	REYNOLDS	Threatened Richard & forced him to leave his good job
IHRCRDA	RICHARD	Black Boy is about him
LONAOS	SALOON	Place where Richard passed time at age 6
LELS	SELL	Richard tried to --- Bessie
YTHROS	SHORTY	Elevator operator
HOTS	SHOT	White men --- Uncle Hoskins
NIMOS	SIMON	Head of the orphanage
FISULN	SINFUL	Granny thought story books were ---
OLSDRSIE	SOLDIERS	Richard saw these & prisoners when returning to Granny's
PECHES	SPEECH	Richard refused to deliver the prewritten graduation -----
MYSLOB	SYMBOL	'My mother's suffering grew into a --- in my mind ....'
NHTKI	THINK	Advice Griggs gave Richard
SHMATO	THOMAS	Richard threatened him with razors
WOLET	TOWEL	Granny hit Richard with one when he told her to 'kiss back there'
DVOOOO	VOODOO	'The ---- of Hell's Half-Acre'
THRIGW	WRIGHT	Author's last name

VOCABULARY RESOURCE MATERIALS

VOCABULARY WORD SEARCH - *Black Boy*

All words in this list are associated with *Black Boy* with an emphasis on the vocabulary words chosen for study in the text. The words are placed backwards, forward, diagonally, up and down. The included words are listed below.

```
P E E R I N G D E B A S E D D E V O I D L G Q B
K E P E O M E T E G N R B S Y E J I E N N I C S
C R T O M R P L Y N N N D N O X V N M I H F E Y
P X B T R U B U S X R I N E T R A A R P S X Z U
J J F U Y M S U D V Y A N N W O E S E E N B H
T J C B E Z O E E E R G E A D T T M V T E T H P
Z N X S F N N N R B N X L Y L I L I N R A P U W
I G S D E G O E B P L T A A O Y T Y F U P T S S
V I N C I T P Y R C W I C L E C A V V L A W E W
D H R E R U S E A M G I P X E Y I W I D V N P D
F A F E G U C P S L T Z P V T N B A I E O P C R
L H V N O O I I A E Z L N E D F B V U B C H D E
Z O A I N T N T H L O I I I M L I G S F B E F H
P N B D U O S T A I D X C M E V I T S B L D Z S
T U I L G O O U T I N T Q T A R I A A U R N Q C
D T A A N P T E V A I D A C T N U F S O J U G T
E T T U Y I D I Q V V L U N A C F I U T A T R B
E N T H R A L L E D U T I C I L O S M L A U Q J
A P P X Z A L F Q M E H Y L E N E F O U O I L D
A V A I L E D R E V E L Y D L D W R T D X S F S
```

ACUTE	DOUR	LARCENOUS	REPUGNANT
ANTAGONISM	DUBIOUS	LIEU	REVEL
ANXIETY	EMULATE	LIVID	RITUAL
ARDENTLY	ENTHRALLED	LOITERING	ROUSED
AURA	EXPLOITED	MOROSE	SAUCILY
AVAILED	FEIGNED	NOSTALGIA	SOLICITUDE
BAFFLED	FIAT	NUANCE	SQUALOR
BOON	FRENZY	OBSTINACY	TAUT
CAPITULATE	HYPOTHETICAL	OVERTONE	VINDICTIVE
CRYPTIC	IMPETUS	PEERING	VIVID
DEBASED	IMPUDENT	PETTY	WANED
DELUSION	INCURRED	PLIABLE	WAYLAYING
DEVASTATED	INDUCED	PRESUME	YEARNED
DEVOID	INTRIGUE	QUALMS	
DISSEMBLE	INVECTIVES	RECONDITE	

VOCABULARY CROSSWORD - *Black Boy*

VOCABULARY CROSSWORD CLUES - *Black Boy*

ACROSS
1. An order or authorization
4. Made use of
10. Completely lacking or empty
14. Imitate
15. Made use of selfishly or unethically
16. A boy had -- in Richard's bed at Uncle Clark's house
17. An ulterior meaning or quality; an implication or hint
18. A single
19. Neither's partner
20. Puzzled; confused
21. Promises
25. Looking intently or searchingly
28. A state of uneasiness and apprehension
30. A state of violent or wild excitement
32. Contraction for I am
33. Cease; halt
34. Clenched hands used for hitting with
35. Heard, seen or felt as if real
37. Harrison and Richard agree to ----
38. Hostility that results in active resistance or oppression
41. To take great pleasure or delight
42. Granny's ally; Richard's teacher
44. Strict Seventh-Day Adventist with whom Richard often lives
46. Sharp or severe; intense
49. Subtle or slight degree of difference
50. Easily influenced or persuaded
51. Acquired

DOWN
2. Making an earnest appeal
3. Also
4. Pretend to be something other than what one is
5. Characterized by strong enthusiasm or devotion
6. In place of
7. Lowered in character, quality or value
8. Doubtful
9. Speaking in a playful or teasing way
10. A false belief or opinion
11. Revengeful
12. An impelling force
13. Public condemnation or censure
20. A benefit
22. Trivial
23. Tending to conceal or camouflage
24. Discolored; showing extreme anger
26. Seeming to be coolly unconcerned or indifferent
27. Suppositional
28. Ambitions
29. Tight; tense
30. Gave a false appearance of; pretended
31. A bittersweet longing for things of the past
36. Set up fight between Richard and Harrison
39. Atmosphere
40. Gloomy
43. Silently ill-humored or sternly obstinate
45. Aunt Addie was Granny's ---
47. Is able to
48. Make a mistake

VOCABULARY CROSSWORD ANSWER KEY - *Black Boy*

	F	I	A	T		A	V	A	I	L	E	D		D		B		D	E	V	O	I	D
D		M		O		C		R		I		E	M	U	L	A	T	E		I		M	
E	X	P	L	O	I	T	E	D		E		B		B		N		L		N		P	
N		L						E		D		A		I		T		U		D	I	E	D
U		O	V	E	R	T	O	N	E			S		O	N	E		S		I		T	
N		R				T						E		U		R		I		C		U	
C		I		B	A	F	F	L	E	D		D		S		I		O	A	T	H	S	
I		N		O		Y				P		C				N		N		I			
A		G		O	L			P	E	E	R	I	N	G				V				H	
T			A	N	X	I	E	T	Y			Y		O			F	R	E	N	Z	Y	
I	M		S		V		A		S	T	O	P		N			E			O		P	
O			P		I		U			Y		T		C		F	I	S	T	S		O	
N		V	I	V	I	D		T		O		F	I	G	H	T		G		T		T	
			R					L				C		A				N		A		H	
			A	N	T	A	G	O	N	I	S	M		L		R	E	V	E	L		E	
			T			U			N		O			A		D				G		T	
A	D	D	I	E		R				G	R	A	N	N	Y			A		I		I	
	O		O		A	C	U	T	E		O			T				L		A		C	
N	U	A	N	C	E		A			R		S		P	L	I	A	B	L	E		A	
	R		S		I	N	C	U	R	R	E	D		Y				Y				L	

VOCABULARY WORKSHEET 1 - *Black Boy*

____ 1. Stubbornness
    A. Obstinacy   B. Fiat   C. Inconceivable   D. Qualms

____ 2. Subtle or slight degree of difference
    A. Boon   B. Taut   C. Nuance   D. Aura

____ 3. Easily influenced or persuaded
    A. Pliable   B. Recondite   C. Predilection   D. Impetus

____ 4. Excited as to anger or action; stirred up
    A. Conspicuously   B. Inconceivable   C. Roused   D. Dissemble

____ 5. Puzzled; confused
    A. Indulgently   B. Baffled   C. Provocations   D. Livid

____ 6. To disguise one's real nature, motives or feelings
    A. Dissemble   B. Denunciation   C. Subservience   D. Squalor

____ 7. Equivalent in effect or value
    A. Tantamount   B. Revel   C. Repugnant   D. Qualms

____ 8. Tight; tense
    A. Repugnant   B. Denunciation   C. Taut   D. Blasphemy

____ 9. Revengeful
    A. Waylaying   B. Vindictive   C. Incurred   D. Lieu

____ 10. Preference
    A. Waylaying   B. Predilection   C. Livid   D. Taut

____ 11. Spellbound; captivated
    A. Solidarity   B. Livid   C. Impetus   D. Enthralled

____ 12. In place of
    A. Lieu   B. Blasphemy   C. Provocations   D. Recondite

____ 13. Completely lacking or empty
    A. Denunciation   B. Larcenous   C. Devoid   D. Availed

____ 14. Tending to conceal or camouflage
    A. Larcenous   B. Repugnant   C. Presume   D. Cryptic

____ 15. Standing idly about; lingering with no purpose
    A. Loitering   B. Predilection   C. Tantamount   D. Saucily

____ 16. A state of uneasiness and apprehension
    A. Squalor   B. Emulate   C. Solidarity   D. Anxiety

____ 17. Sharp or severe; intense
    A. Intrigue   B. Saucily   C. Acute   D. Delusion

____ 18. Approached an end
    A. Loitering   B. Aura   C. Cryptic   D. Waned

____ 19. To take great pleasure or delight
    A. Revel   B. Contemplate   C. Relentlessly   D. Wane

____ 20. A union of interests or purposes among group members
    A. Subservience   B. Cryptic   C. Solidarity   D. Vivid

VOCABULARY WORKSHEET 2 - *Black Boy*

____ 1. OBSTINACY   A. A state of uneasiness and apprehension

____ 2. NUANCE   B. Spellbound; captivated

____ 3. PLIABLE   C. Equivalent in effect or value

____ 4. ROUSED   D. A union of interests or purposes among group members

____ 5. BAFFLED   E. Excited as to anger or action; stirred up

____ 6. DISSEMBLE   F. Approached an end

____ 7. TANTAMOUNT   G. Tending to conceal or camouflage

____ 8. TAUT   H. In place of

____ 9. VINDICTIVE   I. Stubbornness

____ 10. PREDILECTION   J. Completely lacking or empty

____ 11. ENTHRALLED   K. Puzzled; confused

____ 12. LIEU   L. Easily influenced or persuaded

____ 13. DEVOID   M. Sharp or severe; intense

____ 14. CRYPTIC   N. To take great pleasure or delight

____ 15. LOITERING   O. Preference

____ 16. ANXIETY   P. Standing idly about; lingering with no purpose

____ 17. ACUTE   Q. Subtle or slight degree of difference

____ 18. WANED   R. Tight; tense

____ 19. REVEL   S. Revengeful

____ 20. SOLIDARITY   T. To disguise one's real nature, motives or feelings

KEY: VOCABULARY WORKSHEETS - *Black Boy*

Worksheet 1	Worksheet 2
1. A	1. I
2. C	2. Q
3. A	3. L
4. C	4. E
5. B	5. K
6. A	6. T
7. A	7. C
8. C	8. R
9. B	9. S
10. B	10. O
11. D	11. B
12. A	12. H
13. C	13. J
14. D	14. G
15. A	15. P
16. D	16. A
17. C	17. M
18. D	18. F
19. A	19. N
20. C	20. D

VOCABULARY JUGGLE LETTER REVIEW GAME CLUES - *Black Boy*

SCRAMBLED	WORD	CLUE
CUTAE	ACUTE	Sharp or severe; intense
MAANTGISON	ANTAGONISM	Hostility that results in active resistance or oppression
INYTEXA	ANXIETY	A state of uneasiness and apprehension
NERDYLTA	ARDENTLY	Characterized by strong enthusiasm or devotion
TIRASSIPONA	ASPIRATIONS	Ambitions
ARAU	AURA	Atmosphere
LAVDEIA	AVAILED	Made use of
FEBLDFA	BAFFLED	Puzzled; confused
ARETGIBNN	BANTERING	Speaking in a playful or teasing way
MYASHLPEB	BLASPHEMY	To speak of God in an irreverent manner
NOBO	BOON	A benefit
PATUTICALE	CAPITULATE	Surrender; give up
UUSCLSYPIOCON	CONSPICUOUSLY	Obviously
ETNCOMPATLE	CONTEMPLATE	Think about
SUOENPUTTCOM	CONTEMPTUOUS	Scornful
CYTPRCI	CRYPTIC	Tending to conceal or camouflage
ADSBEED	DEBASED	Lowered in character, quality or value
NOLDUSIE	DELUSION	A false belief or opinion
NANDCUOTNIIE	DENUNCIATION	Public condemnation or censure
VADEATTEDS	DEVASTATED	Destroyed
OEDDVI	DEVOID	Completely lacking or empty
SMELDSEBI	DISSEMBLE	To disguise one's real nature, motives or feelings
UROD	DOUR	Silently ill-humored or sternly obstinate
BOSUDIU	DUBIOUS	Doubtful
MELUAET	EMULATE	Imitate
LRDEATNLHE	ENTHRALLED	Spellbound; captivated
LOXDITEEP	EXPLOITED	Made use of selfishly or unethically
EGENIDF	FEIGNED	Gave a false appearance of; pretended
TIFA	FIAT	An order or authorization
RZNEYF	FRENZY	A state of violent or wild excitement
TOYLTIHEPHAC	HYPOTHETICAL	Suppositional
EMIPSUT	IMPETUS	An impelling force
BLACEMPIAL	IMPLACABLE	Impossible to please or satisfy
RNPOIGMIL	IMPLORING	Making an earnest appeal
DUTIPENM	IMPUDENT	Offensively bold
OCNBAEVIECLNI	INCONCEIVABLE	Impossible to comprehend or fully grasp

Black Boy Review Game Clues Continued

MINGTAINNICIR	INCRIMINATING	Causing to appear guilty of a crime or fault
RUCDEINR	INCURRED	Acquired
DEDINUC	INDUCED	Caused
GYNLIDLUNET	INDULGENTLY	Leniently; patiently
GEINTIRU	INTRIGUE	A secret or underhanded scheme
TUTYEVLIIIN	INTUITIVELY	Without the use of rational reasoning; instinctively
CENIESVIVT	INVECTIVES	Abusive language
ENSRACULO	LARCENOUS	Characterized by theft
LEIU	LIEU	In place of
DILIV	LIVID	Discolored; showing extreme anger
GEROTINIL	LOITERING	Standing idly about; lingering with no purpose
SEMOOR	MOROSE	Gloomy
CNYLAHTLNANO	NONCHALANTLY	Seeming to be coolly unconcerned or indifferent
ALGNTAISO	NOSTALGIA	A bittersweet longing for things of the past
UACNNE	NUANCE	Subtle or slight degree of difference
BYSANOTIC	OBSTINACY	Stubbornness
TEVEONOR	OVERTONE	An ulterior meaning or quality; an implication or hint
ZINGNIRAPTO	PATRONIZING	Going to as a customer
NIERPGE	PEERING	Looking intently or searchingly
TYPET	PETTY	Trivial
BELIPLA	PLIABLE	Easily influenced or persuaded
DILOTECPENIR	PREDILECTION	Preference
UERSEPM	PRESUME	Take for granted as being true
RACOOTSINOVP	PROVOCATIONS	Something that incites or is intended to cause trouble
LAQSMU	QUALMS	Uneasy feelings about the rightness of an action
CNTOEREDI	RECONDITE	Not easily understood
TESSEENLLYR	RELENTLESSLY	Steadily; persistently
GETNNUAPR	REPUGNANT	Offensive or repulsive
LEVER	REVEL	To take great pleasure or delight
ITURAL	RITUAL	Ceremony
SOURED	ROUSED	Excited as to anger or action; stirred up
SAYUICL	SAUCILY	Disrespectfully
EEADNTRUS	SAUNTERED	Strolled
LTEDICUISO	SOLICITUDE	Care or concern for the well-being of another

Black Boy Review Game Clues Continued

DIOYRITALS	SOLIDARITY	A union of interests or purposes among group members
RQASOLU	SQUALOR	A filthy and wretched condition
BEENERVSUISC	SUBSERVIENCE	Being subordinate; of a lesser position
RUTTYSOUIRSELPI	SURREPTITIOUSLY	Stealthily
MANTTOUTNA	TANTAMOUNT	Equivalent in effect or value
AUTT	TAUT	Tight; tense
DVIVITEICN	VINDICTIVE	Revengeful
DVIVI	VIVID	Heard, seen or felt as if real
NEWAD	WANED	Approached an end
LAWAYGYIN	WAYLAYING	Ambushing; intercepting someone unexpectedly
NEEDRAY	YEARNED	Had a strong, often melancholy desire

www.ingramcontent.com/pod-product-compliance
Lightning Source LLC
Chambersburg PA
CBHW051414070526
44584CB00023B/3425